ECHOES OF OUR ANCESTORS: THE SECRET GAME

By

James M. Redwine

Echoes of Our Ancestors: The Secret Game

Published by JPeg Ranch

© 2014 James M. Redwine. All rights reserved.

Original Artwork for cover by Cedric Hustace
www.hustaceart.com

ISBN-13:978-0692286319 (JPeg Ranch)

ISBN-10:0692286314

Dedicated to:

My friends from all the tribes with and against whom I played football and other games.

CONTENTS

FOREWORD

The crisp autumn air. The dry brown grass. Sweaty pads and the exhilaration of combat without weapons. The kind of battle where one can experience the thrill of having been shot at and missed without even being shot at. Football. Ersatz war. Clashes of pride, power and cunning.

Americans versus Americans or, as it really happened in 1924 in Osage County, Oklahoma, Native Americans versus the stereotypical Americans, cowboys. Albeit those Native Americans were mainly schoolboys from Haskell Indian Institute and those cowboys were professional football players with the Kansas City Cowboys.

Tiny Haskell Institute with four hundred students from numerous tribes and several states had been beating some of America's best college football teams from Massachusetts to California for several years. But these White powerhouses refused to play at Haskell's makeshift stadium with its packed clay field and non-existent seating. So Haskell's coach, young Frank McDonald, had to stuff his charges and their equipment into automobiles and drive for days to get a game.

In her book *Voices from Haskell, Indian Students Between Two Worlds 1884 – 1928*, Myriam Vuckovic explains the importance of football and a new football stadium to Native Americans in the early 20th Century:

> **"To Haskell's athletes, the football field was a place where they felt they could fight their white opponents on equal terms, proving their intelligence and physical skills. To them, Indian-White football was not just a game. It was about crossing and defending boundaries, history and myth, the frontier, Crazy Horse, and Custer."**
>
> *Haskell* @ **p. 157.**

Vuckovic interprets the funding of the new football stadium at Haskell Indian Institute (1926) by Native Americans, especially oil rich Osages from the new state of Oklahoma, as resulting from:

> **"... [A] great expression of ethnic pride, a place where Indians could symbolically challenge and beat white society."**
>
> *Id.* @ **p. 157.**

Dr. Vuckovic may be correct in her psychoanalysis of Indian motivation. However, as one who grew up on the Osage Nation and played football and poker with Native Americans, I suggest the reasons may have been more prosaic, i.e., the Indians, as Whites, just liked football and gambling.

After Haskell's highly successful 1923 season McDonald conceived of an exhibition game to be played in 1924. His plan was to showcase his Native American players to wealthy Indians in Oklahoma who might then contribute money for an actual stadium.

He set up a game at the high school stadium in Pawhuska, Osage County, Oklahoma, the capital of the Osage Nation. The game was to be between a cobbled together team of local cowboys and oilfield workers whom the Haskell players should find easy to beat. However, once word of the game got out, all manner of grifters, gamblers and con men saw it as an opportunity to separate football and gambling crazy Osages from their oil money.

A team of professionals from Kansas City, the Blues (later the Cowboys), was secretly recruited to play under assumed identities. The panicked Haskell coaches, McDonald and Dick Hanley, with the help of the Principal Chief of the Osages, Fred Lookout, set about getting ringers of their own. Such great players as John Levi, who had just graduated from Haskell, and professionals, even some from the Cowboys, were coaxed into playing for Haskell.

Over two hundred thousand dollars was wagered on the illegal game between college players and professionals that was played at a secret location outside of Pawhuska. Secrecy was required to protect collegiate eligibility and comply with the rules of the nascent National Football League.

This bloody contest became one of the greatest football games to have "never occurred".

PROLOGUE

Coach Frank McDonald shifted his large canvas valise between the seats of his berth in the passenger car of the Atchison, Topeka & Santa Fe Railroad. He stretched his boney legs over the bag and rested the heels of his high button shoes on the seat across from him. He hoped no one would claim the other seat.

Twenty-eight year old McDonald was exhausted after almost four days of negotiating with an assortment of Catholic priests, agents of the Bureau of Indian Affairs, chiefs from various tribes and some of the slickest gamblers in all of the old Indian Territory, the new state of Oklahoma.

After his football teams at tiny Haskell Indian Institute in Lawrence, Kansas had embarrassed major college programs for several years, especially last year, 1923, McDonald had anticipated garnering support for a new stadium would be less problematic. Everyone from whom he sought help extolled the accomplishments of the Indians and wished them future success. No one offered any money.

As McDonald stared out the window at the sea of tall prairie grass with its bluish stems and golden tassels he thought that any randomly selected patch of this sand rock studded sward would provide a better playing surface than the field at Haskell where the rickety stands held less than five hundred spectators and the clay field was either brick hard or slimy depending on the weather.

Last season, All American fullback John Levi had run, passed, kicked and tackled as no other football player in America. But he had to go to Notre Dame, Oklahoma A & M, and football venues from California to Pennsylvania to do so. No teams would come to Haskell to play.

When the nonpareil Jim Thorpe watched John Levi in Minnesota he said Levi was the best football player he had ever seen. And when later that year at a Haskell half-time Thorpe in street clothes stood back to back with Levi at the fifty yard line as they both kicked fifty yard drop-kick field goals and then threw seventy-five yard passes back and forth, the small group of sports writers who observed the Sac-Fox and Arapahoe Indians declared them the greatest athletes in America. However, the field and stadium gained no mention or any calls for improvements.

1924 would be Levi's last season before he turned professional. Jim Thorpe had attended Haskell as a child but performed his collegiate track and field and football heroics at the now closed Carlisle Institute in Pennsylvania. John Levi's brother, George, would return to Haskell for another year.

But now was the time that Haskell was on the front pages of newspapers from coast to coast. The planets were aligned for money to be shaken from awestruck supporters. McDonald had decided the Bureau of Indian Affairs did not want a strong Indian team competing with influential White schools. The epic game at National Champion Harvard had been too close for the Bureau.

McDonald had received the blessing of the priest at the large Catholic Church in the Osage County capital of Pawhuska to solicit funds from the wealthy Osage parishioners. He had met with Father LeMond in the sanctuary that was encircled by expensive stain glass windows commissioned by various Osage families as original works of art. The Stations of the Cross reminded McDonald of his own travails in trying to convince the federal government that Indians deserved more than platitudes. And although several donors had given generously, a great deal more was needed. Therefore, the coach was on his way to meet with the one person whose blessing might bring McDonald's fundraising scheme to fruition.

After years of dealing with White society the Osages were chary about plans that called for the tribe to make deals that always seemed to end up aiding the White men who promoted them at the expense of the tribe. McDonald had already run head on into this attitude in Hominy, Oklahoma with several Osages who questioned why they should finance what the federal government would not. Hominy was only twenty miles from Pawhuska. The tribal leaders there had bad memories of oil and gas get rich quick schemes that had made the schemers wealthy and the Indians poorer. McDonald knew his last best hope was with the Principal Chief of all the Osages, the revered Fred Lookout.

If Chief Lookout could be convinced McDonald's plan was in the tribe's best interest, the chief might be able to get the entire elected Tribal Council to get on board.

Chief Lookout's reputation had been formed when he stood toe to toe with Phillips 66 founder, Frank Phillips, back when Phillips wanted to greatly expand drilling on tribal lands. The two men went from cautious adversaries to close friends and both the company and the tribe were beneficiaries. The coach had not met Lookout but he had heard of his negotiating skills.

McDonald decided he better get some sleep.

Monument to Fred & Julia Lookout
Photo by Peg Redwine

CHAPTER 1 - THE CHIEF OBSTACLE

Frank McDonald carefully guided his new 1959 white Pontiac off the edge of the gravel road at the base of Lookout Mountain three miles east of Pawhuska, Oklahoma. He winced each time he felt the undercarriage scrape across a hidden sand rock and thought how much Chief Fred Lookout would have smugly enjoyed his Whiteman's *beau geste* that was more in the nature of a *mea culpa*.

McDonald thought back to that hot summer thirty-five years ago when Chief Lookout, who was then sixty-three, had led the young football coach up the high rounded dome that provided a panoramic view of the Chief's ranch house, the eight-sided peyote church building below and the town of Pawhuska far away. McDonald's black woolen three piece suit and his new high button thin soled shoes had been no match for the tall dry russet colored prairie grasses, the ubiquitous sand rocks and the voracious chiggers. And young Coach McDonald was no match for the taciturn old Chief who forged steadily upward without seeming to take note of the Whiteman's struggles.

Chief Lookout had not even removed his tall broad brimmed black hat, his knotted white cravat or even his woolen blanket with its stylized eagle pattern. He had kept the blanket clutched in his large sinewy hands that gave evidence of that young man who had long before led the last great buffalo hunt for the Osages.

McDonald slowly exited the Pontiac and gazed up the two dirt tracks that led to the granite stele surrounded by a wrought iron fence without a lock. Respect for the Chief and his beloved wife, Julia, remained so strong no one worried about vandalism. However, thought McDonald, he probably should have more concern for his heart than would be shown by a long trek up to visit the graves of his old friends. He had been too busy to attend Fred's funeral in 1949 or Julia's in 1950, but he hoped this pilgrimage would bring him forgiveness, from himself; he knew the Lookouts would bear him no reproach.

As the setting sun blazed into his eyes he caressed the scalloped edges of the large granite monument and was embarrassed to shed tears in Fred's presence; Julia would understand and approve. Fred would nod and say, "Whiteman", and they would all laugh.

That hot August of 1924 McDonald had planned to carefully present his idea of a fundraising exhibition football game to the Principal Chief of the Osage Nation using charts showing the success of the football team of Haskell Indian Institute. Fred had met him outside as he drove up in the brand new 1924 Ford he had rented but could ill afford. He had hoped to impress the Chief.

"Come", the Chief had said.

Mrs. Lookout had stayed in the house but watched out the front door. McDonald had followed Chief Lookout and tried to talk about his plans. The Chief had kept walking and not talking until they reached the top of the high hill and the Chief had quietly gazed in all four directions. Then he said, "I read your letters. I understand what you want to do. I do not know why it would be good for the tribe." He then walked back down the hill to where Julia waited for them with iced sweet tea.

The young football coach had been devastated but was too much in awe of Chief Lookout to recover his composure. He had mumbled his apologies and prepared to leave until Julia had caught his eye and said, "Would you like to watch the beautiful Osage County sunset on the back porch?"

She had left Fred in the sparsely furnished parlor and led McDonald to the rear of the house.

"May I call you, Frank, Mr. McDonald? I am Julia".

"Of course."

"Frank, my husband has not refused your proposal. He is prone to careful judgment where his people are concerned. Fred and I are both fans of the Haskell football team. We have studied your letters and given a great deal of thought to your idea. I think it might result in a real benefit for the tribe, but Fred is not sure. Let me suggest a different approach. You may know that Fred's braids show he is a follower of both Christianity and the Peyote Church. We are also Catholic. You should know, as you coach Indians, many Indians love to gamble and so do some Catholics. Perhaps you can make use of these factors. Do not give up. Fred appreciates a man who will stand up to him as long as there is respect for our culture.

"Think about these things and please come back for Sunday dinner. Perhaps there is a way to devise what you footballers might call an end around. I like the idea of an athletic contest that showcases the skill of our young men. Of course, our women are not without their own skills. Here is a beaded peyote gourd rattle with red-tailed hawk feathers and an eagle pattern that I made for Fred and had planned to give him at Christmas. Fred is of the Eagle Clan and rightly proud of it. Such a gift would show respect for our people and honor Fred's position. Such protocols are important to Fred. You could present it to him as a gift from your team. Under our traditions such a thoughtful gift would call for a generous response, perhaps a willingness to reconsider your proposal. Someday we will have to confess; maybe after the game."

CHAPTER 2 - THE GIRL AT THE DUNCAN HOTEL

Julia Lookout and Frank McDonald walked from the open back porch down the high steps and around Julia's large sandstone home to Frank's car. Julia had suggested it would be better if Frank did not talk to Chief Lookout again until they could meet over food. She planned to fix Fred's favorite meal of rib eye steak and Indian fry bread with homemade apple butter. And the peyote gourd rattle would be hard to get by Fred.

Frank thanked Julia who said, "Young man, plan as you would for your team to play a big game. Fred has become skeptical of White strangers proposing ways for the Osages to spend money. Concentrate on how your exhibition football game will benefit the tribe, not Haskell Indian Institute or anyone else."

McDonald slowly drove back to Pawhuska with the ceremonial rattle beside his right thigh. He noted the swastika painted in red in the center of the deerskin-covered gourd. There were four red dots, one within each section of the left facing design. The swastika reminded Frank of a bird in flight.

The rattle seemed to follow Frank's gaze when he would glance away from the dirt road to examine it. He felt uneasy alone with this religious symbol miles from town surrounded by prairie. The setting August sun blazed into his eyes that watered as he forced himself to look away from the colorful object so he could avoid the ubiquitous sand rocks in the road.

Frank parked his rented 1924 Ford on Osage Street beside the new Duncan Hotel in Pawhuska. He could see Kihekah (Chief in the Osage language) Avenue running on both sides of the new seven story triangle building in the heart of the town. The county seat gushed with prosperity, energy and opportunity.

Charles and George Duncan had built their hotel only fourteen years earlier and had to expand it with an even more ostentatious addition just last year. The granite entry portico with imported marble flooring accented by an intricate pattern of inlaid ceramic tile spoke of deals to be concocted and fortunes to be made, or lost. McDonald could sense his own excitement and realized Julia's admonishment was necessary.

McDonald took the ceremonial rattle with him and decided to eat supper in the ornate hotel dining room before going to his third floor room. The Negro waiter who was dressed in white livery seated Frank at a small round table facing the atrium filled with plants and flowers that appeared to have been selected because they had no connection to Oklahoma.

Frank ordered a chicken fried steak sandwich and a glass of water. He placed the peyote rattle across from him as though it were a companion.

"That is a marvelous symbol of Wah'Kon-Tah. May I ask where you found it?"

Frank looked up to see an Indian woman with long black hair wearing a red and white flapper type dress with black lace trim. She was about five feet tall and looked to be in her teens. Frank stared at her blankly as he struggled to get to his feet.

"Uh, yes, I mean, that is, it was a gift, but not for me. I mean, it is for me, but to give away. Do I know you?"

"Of course not, we just met. May I sit down?" As she spoke, she sat down with the confidence that she would be welcome. "Would you like to buy me a drink?"

"I don't drink."

"Well, you must get very thirsty. How about a Coca-Cola then?"

Frank called the waiter and ordered two Coca-Colas in the new contour bottles.

"Are you staying at the Duncan? I work here from time to time. Tonight I am just relaxing and looking for conversation. If you don't drink, do you talk? We could discuss your non-gift, gift if you like. Do you understand what the symbols mean?"

"Chief Lookout's wife, Julia, told me the beads were in a stylized eagle pattern, but I imagine there is much more to know."

"Oh, Chief Lookout; you must be somebody. And Julia, on a first name basis already."

"It's not what you may think. I just met them today. The rattle is to be given to the Chief. But, if I may ask, what is it to you?"

"Actually, I am Cheyenne and we and the Osages were traditional enemies. You may know the Osages scouted for Custer

7

when he tracked down Chief Black Kettle of the Cheyenne at the Battle of the Washita. However, that was long ago. Now we are more sanguine in our relationships. Let me tell you about the rattle. Oh, my name is Raven. It used to be Raven That Sings, but that became a bit cumbersome at school. And you are?"

"Frank, Frank McDonald. Please enlighten me."

Original Artwork by Bill Alsabrook & Photography by Richard Stathem
Used by permission from Citizens Bank of Oklahoma
(formerly National Bank of Commerce)
Pawhuska, Oklahoma

CHAPTER 3 – CHIEF LOOKOUT AND THE SWASTIKA

Frank was not comfortable with pretty women. He knew how to motivate young men, but had difficulty participating in conversation if a woman engaged him with her eyes. Raven boldly fixed her bright sloe eyes upon Frank and dared him to meet her gaze; he could not for more than brief moments.

"Mr. McDonald, that peyote rattle is a sacred object to Indians. It symbolizes the universe that is Wah'Kon-Tah. All that there is is Wah'Kon-Tah, a spirit that pervades everything and is everything. Chief Lookout, as many Indians, converted to Christianity because its sense of spirit was similar to traditional beliefs. You see the beaded red crosses on the white beaded handle? Those are not crosses; they represent stars. The color red represents the sun that, much like the Egyptian god Rah, is seen as the source of all life. White is the color of life. The deerskin covered turtle shell holds either bear claws or bear teeth, which together with the hawk feather, stand for the courage shown by Chief Lookout in looking after his people. The buffalo skin covered bois d'arc wood shaft reminds us that we are one with Wah'Kon-Tah that provides us with buffalo and other sustenance.

"The bois d'arc tree is also called the Osage orange. Indian bow and arrow makers prefer it to all other wood. In fact, the Osage orange tree was named the bois (bow) tree by early French trader

Jean Pierre Chouteau after he had observed its use by Indians. You Englishmen should know most Indians preferred the culture-accepting French to the culture-denigrating English."

McDonald squirmed and cast down his eyes. He was used to the monotonal, hesitant speech patterns of young male Indians. He felt inadequate to challenge this beautiful self-assured woman. His confusion clamped his tongue to the roof of his mouth. He decided not to mention that he was Irish, not English, and that the Irish had issues of their own with the British Empire. Further, he suspected the French were no more altruistic than the English, but he found himself just wanting to listen to Raven and occasionally chance a quick look at her face. She knew the effect she had on most men and enjoyed using it to claim equal intellectual status.

"Frank, Frank, are you with me so far? Do you see the swastika in the center of the rattle? That is an ancient symbol of the wish, one might say prayer, for well-being, good fortune as it were. Some Indian tribes may, also, refer to it as the Thunderbird or happiness symbol. The four red dots represent both the four cardinal directions and the four elements: wind, fire, air and water. If you do not oversell your knowledge to Chief Lookout, he may believe you care about the tribe, not just their money. But rest assured he can see through White paternalism and condescension. He has had a lifetime of it."

Frank sensed a harder edge in Raven's voice and noticed now she was the one looking off in the distance. "Thank you, Raven. I knew none of this and am ashamed I didn't after coaching at Haskell for several years. May I ask where you came by your knowledge of these things?"

"I must go now. I have an appointment. Perhaps we will see each other again."

Raven left as effortlessly as she talked. McDonald hardly had time to rise. He called for the Negro waiter and the check as he carefully picked up the sacred rattle. His mind raced through the images of Raven as he exited the dining room. He looked across the large foyer toward the elevator and saw Raven with her left arm through the right arm of a middle-aged White man. Frank's breath caught in his throat as he saw her push the up button.

"What is wrong with me?" he asked himself. "Why is what Raven does any of my business?" McDonald admonished himself as he would his football players to keep his mind on the game and start preparing to do battle with Chief Lookout.

CHAPTER 4 – DADDY WARBUCKS

Coach Frank McDonald stepped into the ornate elevator with its walnut paneling and gold oak leaf inlay surrounding the ceiling. He had hoped to see Raven coming back down, but only the uniformed Colored operator was in the car. Frank started to inquire about Raven and the Whiteman who had just gone up, but turned his curiosity into a cough as he said, "Third floor, please."

The operator turned the metal lever to the number three as he closed the latticed steel door with his other gloved hand. "Suh, does you care to attend de game on de second flo? It be a open game for gentlemen such as yourself."

"What are you talking about? What game?"

"Why, Suh, de card game hosted by Mr. Thompson. Tonight Mr. Cokes is even dere too. You know, de one dey call Daddy Warbucks cause he looks jus like dat new cartoon man from de Annie strip in the *Tulsa World* newspaper."

"I do not gamble; I am a Presbyterian. Third floor, please."

When McDonald got to his room he sat on the white chenille bedspread with its intricate floral pattern and forced himself to study the peyote rattle as he fought to dispel Raven's image. His small window faced Main Street where the glowing gaslights framed passing carriages and the occasional touring car in a blurry glow. Frank filled his fountain pen and made notes on what Raven had told him about the swastika. He knew Chief Lookout would dismiss his entire proposal if it were perceived as just another scheme to

12

separate Osages from their money. In fact, that had been McDonald's plan but only to help build a new football stadium at Haskell Indian Institute. He now knew he had to devise and present a complete outline of a practical idea that benefited both the Osages and Haskell. He realized he had come to the biggest game of his coaching career without a coherent strategy. Maybe he should go back to Kansas and forget the whole thing. But he could not forget Raven.

McDonald rose at four the next morning and did an hour of calisthenics in his room before going for a run. He left the Duncan Hotel and went north up Kihekah Street until he had reached the top of the hills that formed the valley containing Pawhuska. He could barely breathe as he stopped at the Million Dollar Elm where the Osage tribe leased their mineral rights to such oil companies as Phillips Petroleum. His mind was clear of the confusion of the previous night but it also was devoid of any better plan. Maybe he still should just go home.

Frank cooled off by slowly walking down the long brick street that led from the sandstone Osage Indian Agency buildings to the Constantine Theatre then a block east back to the Duncan Hotel. As he entered the hotel lobby he saw Raven with two White men going into the breakfast bar area. He averted his eyes. If she did see him, she could just have her two men. Frank went to his room for a bath and cut himself as he angrily shaved with his pearl handled straight razor.

He could not help himself. He hurriedly dressed in a beige cotton suit with a white shirt and regimentally stripped purple and gold tie, Haskell's school colors. He dabbed his cut chin with toilet paper as he impatiently and repeatedly pushed the down button until the same Colored operator opened the doors.

"Suh, is ya goin' down for breakfast?"

"Yes. Let's go!"

Frank walked up to the frosted cut-glass doors of the breakfast bar and tried to see in without going in.

"Hello, Mr. McDonald. Did you sleep well?" Frank turned to see Raven behind him. "I had to get a *Pawhuska Journal Capital* newspaper. Would you care to join me at my table?"

"Uh, no, well, what about … okay."

"Mr. Frank McDonald, please meet Mr. Hubert Cokes, now known as Daddy Warbucks, and Mr. Alvin Thomas, called by some Titanic Thompson. By the way, Mr. Thomas is my guardian and surrogate father. Frank you look surprised. Perhaps you should remove that piece of tissue paper. I believe these gentlemen may be able to help you with Chief Lookout. If you are interested, please sit down."

CHAPTER 5 – THE HANDS GAME

Alvin Clarence Thomas, a.k.a. Titanic Thompson, stood and extended his right hand that had a diamond ring on the index finger. His French cuff was held with an ivory link carved in the shape of an oil derrick. Thomas wore a three-piece blue serge suit with a thick gold chain and watch fob draping from his vest pocket to his eel skin belt. His matching eel skin shoes glistened in the morning sun which was at Thomas's back and in Frank's eyes. His thick black hair and neatly trimmed sideburns set off his gleaming white teeth with one gold-capped canine. He was five feet ten inches tall and built like a boxer. His gaze challenged Frank who looked down at the table.

When Hubert Cokes stood up he towered over McDonald, Raven and Thomas. He was six foot three inches tall and had no hair on any part of his head. His eyes were small and deep set in his face. This Daddy Warbucks did not strike McDonald as the kindly cartoon character who looked after Orphan Annie. He had an air about him that reminded Frank of a large coiled rattlesnake. When he reached for Frank's hand he cleared the entire table effortlessly. Coke's voice was surprisingly soft as he said, "Raven says you need an edge. Maybe we can help."

With Titanic Thompson and Cokes across the breakfast table, Raven sat next to Frank. Occasionally her left leg would brush against his. He found he could not concentrate on what Thomas and Daddy Warbucks were saying.

Raven said, "Frank, I believe my father and Mr. Cokes might be able to coach you as you might coach your football team. Perhaps you can yet pull off your exhibition game."

"How do you know about my plans? I did not mention them last night at dinner. All we talked about was Chief Lookout and the peyote rattle."

"Frank, this is a small town. Strangers stand out. Besides, Julia Lookout sent me smoke signals after you left her home."

"Smoke signals!"

"Well, actually Julia telephoned me, but you seem convinced we Indians fatten dogs and take scalps. I thought you might accept the smoke thing a little better. Sorry if you are confused. Julia and I are quite close. She helped place me in the St. Louis Girls Boarding School over by Clear Creek and she sponsored me in my confirmation at the Pawhuska Catholic Church. Julia, also, saw that Mr. Thomas took guardianship over me after my parents were killed in a tornado that struck in Dewey, Oklahoma when my parents and I were living there. Dewey is in the county due east of Osage County and about 30 miles from Pawhuska.

"But let's let our two experts advise you on how to beat Chief Lookout at his favorite gambling game, the ancient Indian game of Hands.

"Oh, before we start your Hands Game lessons, let me give you one more Osage religious fact you might get a chance to use when you regale the chief with your knowledge about the peyote rattle. You need to know all Osage religious altars must face west because Osages believe when one dies they travel to Spiritland with Grandfather the Sun, starting at noon. You might have gained this knowledge from the great Osage scholar, John Joseph Matthews, if you had had a chance to meet him. Maybe some day you will. Of course, he may be at Oxford now. Regardless, the altar in the Pawhuska Catholic Church faces west. The Holy Father might not appreciate it but the Osages do.

"Father Thomas, Hubert, he is all yours."

Titanic Thompson spoke first. "Frank, did you hear anything Cokes or I said? Did you notice he and I traded places while Raven was beguiling you? Did you miss your Phi Beta Kappa key from your watch fob? Well, here it is. Get it? You must distract Chief Lookout from a game you are just now learning and he has played since before Custer so unwisely divided his troops at the Little Big Horn.

"But do not panic. Hubert and I are called gamblers, but we do not gamble. We only play to win. Cokes, anything to add?"

"You don't play the game, whatever it is, you play the mark. What angers him? What excites him? What things does he think he knows or cares about more than others do? Let me give you an example. Alvin grew up in Rogers, Arkansas and I grew up in Hot Springs. We're about the same age. When I heard about this hotshot pool player I went to Rogers and studied him. He was great, but he had to have it absolutely quiet when he played. I challenged him to a one hundred dollar per game match of one pocket, and when he agreed I paid a group of laborers to bang on the walls of the pool hall. When he found out I had set him up he was going to shoot me, but we became partners instead.

"From your association with your football players at Haskell Indian Institute you are probably aware many Indians love to gamble. Chief Lookout likes to gamble and is an expert at Hands. Plus he probably assumes, correctly, you aren't. You should be able to draw him into a Hands Game. If you can get a bet that he'll support your plan if you beat him or you will contribute a thousand dollars to the tribal education fund if you don't, then all you have to do is beat him. And, of course, borrow the money from us at ten percent per month interest if you don't. Don't worry; we never break more than one leg at a time. I have an idea or two and so does Ti. By the way, Ti never fell for that noise distraction thing again. In other words, you will only have one chance with the Chief. Let's get to work."

Titanic Thompson   Hubert Cokes

CHAPTER 6 – NEVER GIVE THE CHIEF AN EVEN BREAK

Titanic Thompson said, "Let's adjourn to the poker room on the second floor where we can have some privacy. Our game ended at four this morning after Hubert and I busted six drunk oil men and split the spoils. Raven contributed greatly just by occasionally touching a shoulder of someone with a good hand. Raven needs to tell you about Chief Lookout's interests, strengths and weaknesses so you can distract him during the Hands Game. Julia is already in your camp and will not interfere, although she must play her cards close to her chest. The Chief is nobody's fool and if he suspects a set-up all bets are off. First, Cokes and I will try to coach you in a kind of Statue of Liberty Play. Misdirection is the key."

The four conspirators left the breakfast table and crossed the lobby to the elevator where the Colored operator used a key to let them off on the private second floor. When Frank stepped off the elevator he saw a lavishly decorated hallway leading to a large oak door with a brass viewing port. Thomas opened the door with a key and flipped a light switch just inside the room. A kaleidoscope of sparkling crystals refracted the light from a huge chandelier hanging over an octagonal table in the center of the room. There was green felt covering all but the mahogany chip and drink holders in front of each of the eight positions. Each position had a cushioned armchair. Two of the chairs had brass plates in the center of the front side of the chair backs. These chairs were directly across from one another.

Both plates were engraved, one with "Mr. Thomas" and the other with "Mr. Cokes".

"Frank, the start of the Hands Game is played with one buckeye for each player. First, stakes are agreed upon, then, for the preliminary stage, both players take a buckeye and put both of their hands behind their backs. On the simultaneous count of one, two, three both players bring both of their hands in front of them with the palms down. Of course, the buckeye will be in one of each player's hands. The players guess which hand their opponent's buckeye is in by simultaneously saying their guesses. The first player to get two-in-a-row correct gets to choose whether he will be the one who holds the buckeye or the one who guesses which hand it is in when the actual game starts. You should let Chief Lookout guess right the first two times and you should try to guess wrong. Your first objective is to encourage the Chief to believe he can tell which hand your buckeye is in. We want you to be in control of the buckeye. Hubert, what is your plan for achieving this outcome?"

"Coach, let's talk about how you get Lookout to win the first part so he is encouraged to have you be the one who holds the buckeye. Expert Hands players know beginners normally avert their eyes from the hand the buckeye is in. Do not be too obvious, but in addition to manipulating the buckeye as you should, try to get the Chief to believe you are giving away your position. If you can get him to believe he has figured you out, he will want to be the one who chooses and he will want you to be the one who holds the buckeye.

"Normally you would use two buckeyes to pull off a Hands Game con. For hundreds, maybe thousands of years, Indians have dealt with buckeye manipulators just as card sharks do cards. For example, when Ti and I play poker, each time Ti draws an ace he uses the roughed underside edge of his index finger ring to mark a corner. Then we never stay in a hand if we are sure someone else has an ace, unless we have drawn something strong. This is usually just enough of an edge to change the odds. During several hours of poker this slight advantage is all Ti and I need when coupled with our brother-in-lawing and secret signals.

"Our plan will work better if you can get the Chief to agree to use small glass beads instead of buckeyes. Manipulation of these beads will be much easier than buckeyes.

"But how do you manipulate the beads or buckeyes? Ti and I have devised a system that calls for cool nerves and distraction. Look at this device we concocted from crimp cut Camel tobacco bags. We will pin a bag just inside the cuff of each of your shirtsleeves. The Chief may demand you take your coat off. You must wear a dark shirt. You will notice we have colored both bags with black ink. Raven found some strong thin black thread that we used to replace the drawstrings of the bags. The thread goes around the little finger of each hand. I will loan you rings for your fingers that will hide the thread.

"Come on, Frank. Don't look so scared. What's the worst that will happen? If you don't pull this off, you will be just where you were before. That is, the Chief won't support your plan. Oh, there is that matter of owing us a thousand, but let's take one thing at a time.

"Here's how it works. Each time you will take a bead or buckeye from both of your two hip pockets so you have one in each hand when you bring them in front. You will start with several beads or buckeyes in each back pocket. Wear extra large pants. Do not wear Levis or any other coarse material. Buy a pair made from some slick, stretchy material like gabardine. You want the back pocket openings real wide. Now we will go to how you will win the actual game.

"If the Chief indicates your left hand, you will palm the bead, hopefully, or buckeye into the bag and show him your right which will have a bead in it. During this entire encounter you must distract him with conversation, hand and body motions and especially eye movement. If you can get him talking, that is your best cover. You will have to show both hands, but do not extend either pinky. Practice curling them under while extending your other fingers.

"Normally, the Hands Game is played best two out of three. Don't take chances. The less time you play, the less chance he will have to catch you. Try to win the first two.

"Of course, he may choose to have you guess while he holds the buckeye. Should that happen, you can be assured he won't cheat but he will most certainly try to outsmart you. We will practice techniques you can use for this too. For example, even the best Hands or poker players cannot control their pupils or their nostrils when excited. You can act like you're going to pick one hand then back away while watching the Chief's face. If his pupils grow larger or his nostrils flare, pick the other hand. You have three tries. If the hand you choose doesn't contain the bead, you know what to look for the next two times. If it does, you only have to repeat your tactic to win. Ti, anything else?"

"Frank, we will practice in this room all day today and every day the rest of this week if you want. Cokes and I must run our game at night. Meantime, Raven can give you inside information on Chief Lookout. Would it be okay with you to spend the next few early evenings with Raven? That's kind of you, Frank."

CHAPTER 7 – PAY ATTENTION

"Raven, leave us men alone for awhile. Mr. Cokes and I must concentrate on Coach McDonald's conditioning. Perhaps you and Frank can go see the new play at the Constantine this evening, but please be back for the game starting at nine p.m. Frank, you had best plan on getting to bed early because tomorrow will be more intense than today."

Raven kissed Thomas on the cheek and lithely walked out of the room like a mountain lion with hunting on her mind. Frank could not help but watch her until she passed through the door.

"All right, Hubert, hook our young friend up with your two bag invention."

Cokes slipped a Camel tobacco pouch past the cuff of each of Frank's sleeves and rolled a thin loop of strong thread around the first joint below the nail of each of Frank's little fingers then covered each loop with a large oblong ring. Next he gave Frank six buckeyes and six red beads for his two hip pockets.

"We hope the Chief will go for the beads, but you must practice both ways. Okay, Frank, what have you already done wrong?"

Frank stared into Cokes' dead grey eyes and was unable to respond until Titanic Thompson said, "You look like a school boy who got caught shooting paper wads. Speak up and look up! Are you listening to me?"

Frank knew how his football players felt at practice. "Uh, I don't know. I just put the beads and buckeyes in my pockets."

"Yes, but you put them all together so you might choose the wrong one and are you deaf? Didn't you hear them clash together? Do you think maybe Chief Lookout could hear them too? Take a couple of these table napkins until you can get two silk handkerchiefs and separate the beads from the buckeyes and cushion both with the extra material. Now you must practice feeling the difference with both hands."

Hubert Cokes stuck out his right hand and said, "That's okay, Frank, let's start over with a handshake. No, no, no! Do not extend all four fingers. Lookout might feel the thread or it might break or come loose from the bag. Are you trying to lose a thousand dollars? Do you really want to owe **us** money? Here, shake hands with your little finger curled under. If you are afraid the Chief might get suspicious, grab his right hand with both of your hands making sure to keep your little fingers bent. Let's try it again."

Thomas opened both Camel tobacco pouches and said, "Now, Frank, practice closing both bags by extending your fingers. No! Extend your little fingers completely out so the bag closes and no beads or buckeyes escape. No! Extend it out under the next finger so no one can see it being extended and so the thread doesn't show. Cokes, you better take over before I get violent."

"Coach, why don't you practice opening the bags while your hands are in your hip pockets and then emptying them into the pockets. During that same operation you need to bring the open empty bags back out of your pockets. Do it as Ti showed you. Just relax and concentrate on those few simple moves. That's it; try it again.

"Say, are you a baseball fan? I figured you might be since you're a coach. Remember Shoeless Joe Jackson and the 1919 World Series between the Chicago White Sox and the Cincinnati Reds? You know those crooks Arnold Rothstein and Abe Attell are the ones who set up Jackson and made a fortune betting against him. Did you know Shoeless Joe hit for the highest average of any player on either team and he didn't commit one error? And in spite of a jury clearing Jackson, Judge Kenesaw Mountain Landis, when he became the new Commissioner of Baseball, banned Joe for life. Some judge he is. But Rothstein's the one Ti and I plan to make pay for ruining Joe's career and life. The fact we bet big on the Sox didn't help either. We'll see Rothstein gets his someday.

"Oh, by the way, you just dropped two beads and one buckeye on the Persian rug. You think maybe the Chief will have your scalp? Pay attention to your task; do not fall for the misdirection. That is what you are supposed to learn from Raven to use against Lookout. Let's do it again."

CHAPTER 8 – OUT OF BREATH

Raven and Frank walked west along Main Street from the Duncan Hotel to the Constantine Theatre a block away. The marquee announced a touring vaudeville show. Frank was afraid to reach for Raven's hand, but he did feign to protect her by getting as close as he could while negotiating them through the large crowd in line for tickets. He knew he would not be able to talk to Raven in the theatre and the show was supposed to be two hours long. After the show Raven would just have time to get back to the Duncan for the nine o'clock game. Frank wanted to get Raven alone but he could not bring himself to suggest they not go to the show.

"Frank, I do not care for vaudeville. It is a little too ribald and slapstickish for my tastes. Do you mind if we just get an ice cream and walk for a while? Besides, aren't you supposed to be mining me for inside information on Chief Lookout?"

"I like black walnut ice cream. What do you want, Raven?"

"Chocolate is my weakness. Make mine a double dip cone. That way I'll be sure and drip it all over my new dress Father Thomas bought me." Frank bought the ice cream at the confectionary beside the Constantine. He asked for several extra napkins.

"I see there is a Tom Mix movie on across the street at the new State Theatre. Isn't Mix from your old hometown of Dewey? Would you want to take that in?"

Frank immediately chastised himself. Here Raven had given him the perfect opportunity to talk with her yet he blew it by trying to impress her with his knowledge of Tom Mix.

"Yes, Tom is from Dewey and his head hasn't got too big for his movie Stetson. He comes home regularly, rides in the Dewey Rodeo and leads the parade."

Frank's heart sank.

"But I can see Tom almost anytime he comes home. Let's walk and talk and enjoy our ice cream."

Frank asked, "Are you game for a walk up Grandview Avenue to the top of the hill where the Million Dollar Elm is? We can take our time; talk as we walk and try to eat our cones before they melt all over us. It might be a little strenuous."

"I'll show you strenuous!" Raven jogged across Main Street then started up the long brick road to the Osage Indian Agency. Frank raced past her then jogged backwards up Grandview while facing down the hill and taunting the panting Raven.

"Okay, Uncle, slow down, you win. But I think we both lost most of our ice cream."

"Raven, there's something I want to ask you when we get to the top of the hill. For now, let's just keep climbing."

After fifteen minutes of hiking straight up Grandview Avenue they reached the Million Dollar Elm then flopped down. Raven was trying to catch her breath as she struggled to get out, "What … what did you … want to ask … me?"

"Would you go with me when I see Chief Lookout and would you care to go out on a real date with me, say to Bartlesville to a Phillips Sixty-Sixer professional basketball game this weekend? Do you like basketball?"

"I have to help Father and Hubert Saturday night, but maybe I could go Sunday afternoon if they are playing. Yes, I like basketball and even played it at college. Father Thomas sent me to Bryn Mawr in Pennsylvania where I studied girls six on six half-court basketball and pretended to attend class. So, yes, it worked, but it almost did you no good as I thought I was going to die.

"Now that your scheme has worked on me we better start your education about how to distract Chief Lookout. And it probably will help if I go with you but I will have to bring Julia in on everything. I cannot mislead her. She is like a second mother to me. Of course, she already believes an Indian versus White football game could be good for not only Osages but all Indians if Haskell wins or, at least, is not embarrassed. Also, Julia will not want to mislead Fred for very long, so if you get his support by slight of hand we will very soon have to come clean with him too. The delicate part will be how Father Thomas and Hubert react. You'd better leave it up to me when and how we tell them. You understand Father and Mr. Cokes are only interested in your plan because they see a huge gambling opportunity involving wealthy oil men and ranchers, Indian and White. They will not take kindly to anything that interferes with their chance to make money.

"Now, as to Chief Lookout, one thing that might surprise you is he is very patriotic. Many Indians feel that way. Fred is quite proud of the Osages and other Indians who served in the great World War. One of our heroes is the famous scholar I mentioned before, John Joseph Mathews. He was an army pilot and even taught other soldiers to fly. Mathews is a local Osage boy who got his early education in Pawhuska then went on to Oklahoma University and Oxford. Another plus for your plan is Mathews graduated from Pawhuska High School in 1914 and was the captain of the football team. It should be easy to get Chief Lookout talking about John Joseph Mathews.

"On a personal note, the Chief and I are close. You might mention I was saved from that tornado and fire in Dewey by a little neighbor girl, Clarice Berryhill.

"Clarice and her family lived just down a country lane from my parents and me. Clarice was only six years old at the time but she was helping my mother and me cook and clean for a dollar a week. My mother was far along in her pregnancy and was having difficulty. Mother and I needed help with the house so I could concentrate on caring for her. Clarice would get to our home at four a.m. each day to start breakfast. The morning of the tornado it was quite cold and my father had kept a fire in the kitchen stove until we went to bed. He thought it was out, but the firemen believe the wind from the tornado made it flare up and ignite a coffee can filled with bacon grease my mother kept on the stove.

"We only had one bedroom and that's where my parents slept. I slept on the enclosed back porch. When Clarice got to our house the winds were howling and the house was already ablaze. She woke me and led me off the back porch but the rest of the house was destroyed in minutes. There was no possible way to save my parents. Clarice and I huddled together in a ditch until the tornado passed and help arrived.

"The Lookouts knew the Berryhills and right away the Chief and Julia took me in until Father Thomas became my guardian.

"Chief Lookout will readily respond to questions about me, Dewey, Tom Mix and Clarice.

"Well, that should be enough for you to build a misdirection ploy on. I don't like fooling Chief Lookout, but, if Julia thinks it will be best in the long run, I'm okay with it."

CHAPTER 9 – NO PRESSURE

In the early morning hours of a particularly hot day during the particularly hot August of 1924 Frank McDonald lay on his bed in the Duncan Hotel on the Osage Indian Nation in Pawhuska, Oklahoma and tried to understand how his plan to raise money for a new football stadium for Haskell Indian Institute had careened out of his control. All he wanted was a decent place for his young Indian football players to showcase their exceptional accomplishments. Yet, now he was practicing how to deceive Chief Lookout with the help of two professional gamblers who were only interested in making money for themselves.

After three long days of practicing how to cheat his way to the Chief's support for an exhibition football game, Frank's fear of Titanic Thompson and Daddy Warbucks Cokes was competing with a feeling of self-loathing. Is this the type of behavior he wanted from his players? He talked with his players of character and honor and self-respect in an America where Indians were second-class citizens in their own country but his own behavior gainsaid his words. Even if he were successful in conning Chief Lookout, a highly questionable outcome, what lie would Frank have perpetrated?

Earlier that day he had tried to talk about his concerns with Titanic and Cokes but they had made sure Frank saw the pistols they carried as they talked about other deals that had gone bad when they had been double-crossed. With Frank's appointment with Chief

Lookout only a few hours away he faced a choice between going along to get along or doing the harder right.

Then there was Raven. Frank knew much of his difficulty was a result of his feelings for her. He was not completely naïve. He knew Alvin Thomas and Hubert Cokes purposefully put him with Raven to get what they wanted, that is, control of Frank. What he did not know was whether Raven was complicit in their scheme. Was he fooling himself into believing their vigorous walks and quiet talks were fun for her too? What's in her heart? More importantly to Frank was, what's in her character? Was she a reluctant participant trying to please her father or was she just another shill?

Frank practiced the Hands Game tricks more than a thousand times and surprised himself by how facile he had become at manipulating the buckeyes and beads. He enjoyed mastering the skill much as he enjoyed learning and teaching new football techniques. His mind only occasionally made him admit these were ways to break the rules. He even had gotten fairly adroit at talking about football and the Great War and the 1919 World Series to misdirect the Chief's attention. Frank almost had himself convinced he could deceive the Chief. His problem was he felt if he won the Hands Game by slight of hand he would lose more than he could gain.

After a sleepless night he sat up on the edge of his bed and looked out the hotel room window at the man delivering large cans of milk to the hotel kitchen. His gray cotton uniform showed large patches of perspiration as he struggled with the heavy containers in the morning heat that was already nearing 85°. What he was not wrestling with was his conscience. At that moment the milkman's job looked appealing to Frank.

If this were a football situation, how would he analyze it? Unfortunately, this was not a game. Hubert Cokes and Alvin Thomas were real. Raven seemed more like a dream. He feared the gamblers and feared losing Raven, if he ever had her to begin with. He feared being unmasked by Chief Lookout. He feared what his players would think about him if they found out. Most of all he feared how he would feel if he engaged in such deceit.

In a few hours he had to meet Titanic and Cokes for a final run through. Then he and Raven had to go to dinner at the Lookouts' home just east of Pawhuska. He felt as he always did just before a kickoff. His stomach was hollow except for the nausea caused by the huge butterflies. There was no relief in sight. His hour was at hand. Perhaps breakfast would help. No, no food; he feared he couldn't keep it down.

Could he confide in Raven or would she think him weak? What if he simply stood up to Thomas and Cokes? What would they do? On the other hand, if he did not deceive the Chief would he be letting his team down? Maybe he would be cowardly if he did not go through with the scheme. And, if he didn't, how would Haskell ever get a stadium? Or was this truly one of those situations where the end justified the means? After all, Julia Lookout thought it was in the tribe's best interest to have the game and she was willing to help with the peyote rattle, although Frank doubted Julia would approve of cheating. Anyway, many things in life are gray. Almost nothing is all white or all black. Perhaps the greater good called for some situational ethics. Where did his true duty lie? Frank's head hurt.

CHAPTER 10 – CIRCLE THE WAGONS

Chief Fred Lookout, his wife, Julia, Raven and Coach Frank McDonald sat on the veranda of the Lookout ranch house in the early evening of July 4, 1946 and watched as Osage boys shot off fireworks that lit up the tallgrass prairie. Several cowboys stood ready with wet gunnysacks in case of a misadventure. It had been a wonderful feast day in celebration of the country's birth but especially for the end of World War II.

Speeches by Chief Lookout and several politicians were interspersed among the horse races, baseball games and barbeque. After four years of war and a quarter of a million Americans killed, the country was ready for a respite from sacrifice and fear.

"Fred, do you remember how I had planned to impress you with my supposed knowledge of Osage lore when I presented you with that peyote rattle in 1924? Of course, Julia had actually made it and loaned it to me in aid of my nefarious plot to get your support for the Indian-White football game. Julia, Raven and I thought we were being quite clever in having me point out the ancient swastika good luck symbols."

"I knew Julia was working on the rattle as a gift for me but didn't let on. When you showed up with it I knew there was something amiss. Julia had been trying to change my mind about supporting the game, but I feared it would turn out badly for the Indians as most plans by White men had. I didn't trust you; I was right!"

Frank, Julia, Raven and the Chief laughed as one.

"True, Fred, but Raven's guardian, Titanic Thompson, and that con man, Hubert Cokes, were playing all of us. That scheme they devised to cheat you in the Hands Game might have actually worked if I had had the nerve to go through with it. I was never so glad when Raven and I showed up for dinner at your place that Sunday afternoon and the first thing you said was, 'Julia says I should support your game.'"

Raven was still laughing as she said, "Well, what I remember most from that day, other than you sweating through your dark shirt, was when Fred said, 'Coach McDonald, you appear to have something in your back pockets,' and you almost fainted as you tried to explain the bulging buckeyes and beads. When you pulled out those two silk handkerchiefs I was impressed. Apparently your training from Ti and Hubert wasn't entirely wasted."

"My young friends, those were good days. 1924 was after the Great War, before the Great Depression and before our most recent War to End All Wars. Then we Indians could use our beloved swastikas. You remember that Oklahoma's 45th Infantry Division, the Indian Division that fought bravely at Sicily and many other places in Europe, used to have the swastika as its shoulder patch until 1939 when that paperhanging Austrian stole it for the Nazis.

"When Clarice Berryhill's younger brother came back from his heroics at Anzio, he and I talked about how the 45th had to change to the Thunderbird emblem to avoid confusion in battle. Bill was about as angry at Hitler for that as he was for having to fight the German soldiers (when America finally got into the war)."

Julia Lookout had listened quietly as her husband reminisced. "Fred, when did you change your mind about supporting the exhibition football game between Haskell and the White cowboys and oilmen? You didn't tell me until you told Frank."

"Actually, I had been approached by Raven's guardian and Cokes in the Smokehouse billiards parlor the day before we all met here. Titanic Thompson told me he thought if the game were properly promoted we might be able to raise several thousand dollars to help build the Indians at Haskell a real stadium instead of that rock pile they were using. He had a betting scheme in mind that involved Arnold Rothstein and several wealthy White oilmen from Tulsa and elsewhere. He promised me there would be no need for the tribe to invest its own money. He and Cokes said they would pay the tribe five thousand dollars cash up front if the game could be played within the boundaries of the Osage Reservation where the federal government would have no jurisdiction over the gambling. I told them I had to take the matter to the Tribal Council. I did so the night before we got together. The Council voted to approve the sponsorship of the game but I had not had time to tell Thomas and Cokes.

"I confess I enjoyed watching you nervously maneuver around what was supposed to be a set up of me. On the other hand, I could have simply let you try to pull off the slight-of-hand and then told you. No, no, don't thank me."

"Okay, you got me. I deserved it for flying false colors. I should have known Ti and Hubert would hedge their bet on my ability to con you in the Hands Game. But tell us, how did a simple little exhibition football game turn into a $200,000 bonanza and a new stadium for my team?"

CHAPTER 11 – THE DRILL FIELD

Frank McDonald walked from his quarters in the staff building to the central drill area that also served as the football field. Haskell Indian Institute's student body of four hundred, half of whom were female, was being rousted out at six a.m. by a bugle call. By six-thirty they would be in formation.

The regimen of imposed Anglo time, the cutting of hair, prohibition of tribal languages and Christianization were the building blocks of assimilation. It would be years before Frank gave more than passing thought to these procedures. In 1924 Frank's Irish ancestry found no problem with trying to save the students from their native culture.

What was on Frank's mind, other than Raven, that early September morning was meeting with his fellow coach, Richard Hanley, to bring him up to date on his efforts to set up the exhibition football game and jump-start the fund drive for a new stadium. Technically, any stadium would not be a replacement as the Indians played their games on the bare clay with rickety bleachers.

McDonald and Hanley worked well together. Hanley had been a star halfback for Washington State University and played on the team that defeated Brown University in the 1916 Rose Bowl. Hanley knew football and could coach it although his strict disciplinarian manner often put him at odds with the more sanguine McDonald. Hanley subscribed to the theory that tolerance led to disrespect and disrespect of the coach led to losing on the field.

McDonald found the Indian students' difficulty complying with White expectations understandable albeit frustrating.

When a player would sneak away to the nearby Wakarusa River to hunt or fish or smoke or meet a girl Hanley would impose harsh penalties, such as extra mopping of floors or removal of privileges. McDonald, who was also the Athletic Director and, officially, Hanley's superior, would temper the sanctions while soothing Hanley's ego with assurances the Indians would play better football if they were punished with extra drills.

McDonald and Hanley surveyed the parade ground/football field after the students had been marched to breakfast. It was no wonder that their football team had to travel back and forth across America and spend weeks away from Haskell to get teams such as Minnesota, Boston College, Brown, Xavier, Tulsa, Oklahoma, Oklahoma State and Creighton to give them a game. The only teams that would play at Haskell were junior colleges or clubs. Even Kansas and Kansas State refused to play at Haskell.

Before each practice and every game the coaches would line the players up and have them scour the field for rocks or rubbish. Then lime lines would be applied. At least the administration allowed the crude wooden goal posts to remain up. Of course, the students reveled in tearing them down after each game since Haskell virtually always won.

"Frank, how did it go down on the Osage Nation? Do you think those rich Osages will help our kids who come from tribes from Alaska to North Carolina?"

"It was quite interesting. It looks like our exhibition game is on for the Pawhuska High School stadium at the end of the season, probably over Thanksgiving or near Christmas. Our opponent will be a team of White cowboys and oil field workers from the nearby town of Fairfax. We should be able to showcase our boys without too much chance of a serious challenge."

"Frank, when are we going to get a bus for all this traveling? And what about bleachers? Heck, there's no place for people to sit! It's a good thing we only have four hundred students."

"Dick, I guarantee you we will have a real stadium some day if we have to build it ourselves. We have been one of the best college football teams in the country for more than ten years and even the great Jim Thorpe said just last year that our full-back, John Levi, Big Skee as the students call him, is the best athlete in America. We need, deserve and will get that stadium!"

McDonald decided not to mention the involvement of Titanic Thompson and Hubert Cokes. "There would come a time for such a thought."

42

CHAPTER 12 – JIM THORPE AND JOHN LEVI

Haskell Indian Institute Coach and Athletic Director Frank McDonald and Head Football Coach Dick Hanley kicked off the stadium fund drive during the season's first game between Still Community College of Northern Iowa and Haskell on September 23, 1924. Still College was small but fielded an experienced team, although Haskell won easily. The most important factor to McDonald and Hanley was that Still College was willing to play on Haskell's field because its own facility was not much better than Haskell's. McDonald and Hanley wanted to use the home half-time show to raise the first contributions for the new stadium.

In 1923 Haskell's all-purpose fullback, John Levi, had been selected as an All-American even though the only significant exposure he had received in front of the influential eastern sportswriters was in Haskell's games against the University of Minnesota, Boston College and an exhibition game against a team of United States Marines. The Fighting Indians and the Marines played in Yankee Stadium. Jim Thorpe sat on Haskell's bench during the Minnesota game and after watching John Levi run, pass and kick said, "John Levi is the greatest athlete I have ever seen".

Frank McDonald took the opportunity to invite Thorpe back to Haskell. Thorpe had attended Haskell as a youngster before leaving for Carlisle Indian Institute in 1904. Thorpe and McDonald planned to surprise the crowd with an exhibition of the passing and dropkicking skills of Thorpe and Levi.

On that bright September afternoon the crowd first saw a snake dance by Haskell's female students wrapped in red blankets. Then they were joined by members of the football team in their uniforms adorned with feathers and wearing headdresses. Accompanied by sounds of several large calfskin-headed drums beating out a pulsating rhythm, the "wild Indians" danced and yelled as the crowd lead by the students chanted, "Indians, Indians, Indians!"

With the charged atmosphere at its peak John Levi doffed his large headdress and stood on the fifty-yard line facing the west goal post. Then McDonald used a megaphone to announce, "Ladies and Gentlemen, please welcome one of Haskell's most illustrious returning sons, the great Jim Thorpe!"

As Thorpe, wearing a Haskell jersey and street clothes, jogged to midfield to stand back to back with Levi, the crowd worked itself into a frenzy of yelling and foot stomping.

With fellow footballers handing each man footballs, Thorpe and Levi first made several fifty yard drop-kick field goals then played catch while running back and forth along the two twenty yard lines.

When the crowd quit yelling and applauding after Thorpe and Levi shook hands at the fifty yard line, McDonald introduced United States Senator Charles Curtis of Kansas who handed McDonald his personal check as the ceremonial first contribution to the stadium fund. McDonald would later wryly comment to Hanley they were now only almost one hundred percent from their goal.

Meanwhile, back in Osage County, Oklahoma Titanic Thompson and Daddy Warbucks Cokes were carefully planning to ensnare Arnold Rothstein in their scheme of an off the books football game. But unbeknownst to them, Rothstein was surreptitiously weaving a nefarious web of his own, much as he had in the 1919 World Series.

CHAPTER 13 – AS YE SOW...

Alvin (Titanic Thompson) Thomas and Hubert (Daddy Warbucks) Cokes were getting excited. For two small town boys from Arkansas they were living large. Their team play during the Saturday night poker game at the Duncan Hotel on the Osage Nation was almost too easy to be fun. The cattlemen and oilmen drank too much, did not study the odds and had money. The oilmen were especially ripe for the plucking as their money came almost miraculously and in large, surprising spurts. Chasing an inside straight or betting on the come was about the same as wildcatting for oil.

As that lovely autumn of 1924 turned the tall prairie grasses to russet and the blackjack oaks to wind chimes of rustling brown leaves, Titanic and Hubert sat on a sandstone ledge by a golf course on the high hill that formed the southwestern edge of Pawhuska. Far across the valley they surveyed the bustling county seat with its pretentious granite courthouse next to the native sandstone buildings of the Osage Indian Agency.

"Hubert, you ever play golf?"

"No, there wasn't much call for it in Rogers, Arkansas."

"The reason I wanted us to drive up here this morning is I have a plan to draw Rothstein here before the football game. We have already made sure he's aware of the game, so we know he won't be able to pass up a chance to bet on it. But, I want to get him here soon and start working on his outsized ego and his undersized ability. He fancies himself a golfer; however, he plays golf just like he does everything else. If he can't fix it, he can't win. I believe we can salt the mine a little and make him think he has an edge to beat me. We have played in California and New York where I have always allowed him to stay close but never win. I usually control my score with putting.

"Look around you, Hubert. This little nine-hole course we are looking at has something Arnold Rothstein has probably never heard of, sand greens. Since there's little water in Oklahoma they can't keep grass greens. Let's walk over to that green perched on the side of this hill and I'll show you how it works.

"A golfer just has to get his ball on the sand then mark it, pick it up and use these little metal rollers to make a putting lane to the hole. Then you empty the sand out of the hole and putt along the lane you just rolled. It's almost impossible to need more than two putts and it is impossible for a ball to not stick on the green from the fairway.

"I plan to contact Rothstein and offer to play him here for $1,000 a hole for eighteen holes or for as many as he wishes with a side bet of another $1,000 per hole that I can two-putt each hole and a third side bet that I will not have an approach shot hit a green then roll off. What do you think?"

"Ti, I think golf is about as dumb a game as was ever concocted by the Devil. However, we both know Rothstein. The dollar signs will dance all over his eyes and he'll probably arrive in Pawhuska next week if he has to ride the caboose of the Atchison,

Topeka and Santa Fe. Maybe it will be the start of our revenge for Shoeless Joe and the 1919 World Series.

"But, say, Ti, what about your bet this morning that you could throw that sunflower you took out of the floral display in the lobby of the Duncan Hotel up on the roof of the hotel? That befuddled oilman couldn't believe you actually lobbed that thing three stories high. How'd you do it?"

"Hubert, yesterday evening I paid that Colored porter five dollars to switch one of the four sunflowers in the display with one I had imbedded with a few buckshot. This morning I just picked that one as if at random. It was an easy $500. The hard part was picking out a mark at breakfast and suckering him in. I hope Rothstein falls as easy.

CHAPTER 14 – MOTHS TO THE FLAME

Haskell's Fighting Indians hosted Midland Nebraska Lutheran College October 25, 1924 (won 28 to 9). But the games against Still College from Iowa (won 12 to 0) and Midland were its only home games. The rest of that season Coaches Frank McDonald and Richard Hanley stuffed their twenty-five players into a caravan of private automobiles driven by the coaches and players and traveled across America looking for schools to play.

Because Haskell had dominated colleges from California to New York for several years, opponents were hard to find. Well-established programs had little to gain from playing a tiny all Indian school from Kansas. Besides, there was a distinct possibility the Indians would win. In order to get games the team played upon the White society's stereotypes of the savages. Headdresses, feathers, stomp dances and war whoops were de rigueur to appease the White fans. This allowed the White schools to believe they were only doing their Christian duty and assuaged their egos if they lost. However, it made for long tiring travels and long absences from class.

The Indians drove to the University of Minnesota October 11, 1924 (lost 0 to 20), then back to Tulsa University October 18 (won 26 to 3), then home for Midland. November 1 Haskell tied Creighton University at Omaha, Nebraska (7 to 7). November 8 they played Brown University in Providence, Rhode Island (won 17-13), then lost to Boston College 7 to 34 on November 22 before traveling to Indianapolis to beat Butler University 20 to 7 on November 29 and Xavier University in Cincinnati, Ohio on December 8 (won 47-6).

As the team was driving to Muskogee, Oklahoma from Cincinnati to play Oklahoma Baptist College (won 55 to 0) on December 15 Frank McDonald pondered how the Fighting Indians could continue traipsing across America in pursuit of games. He vowed to himself there would be a home stadium for Haskell and the upcoming exhibition game in Pawhuska, Oklahoma would be the catalyst.

Meanwhile Titanic Thompson and Hubert Cokes were cautiously preparing Arnold Rothstein for plucking. But Rothstein had been working on a plan of his own ever since he got wind of the exhibition game between Haskell Indian Institute and a makeshift assortment of amateur White cowboys and oilfield workers.

As Thompson and Cokes relished making Rothstein pay for fixing the 1919 World Series on which they had lost thousands, Rothstein was contacting his friends in Kansas City who owned the professional football team called the Kansas City Cowboys. Their season would be ending just in time for the exhibition game in Pawhuska and they were eager to do battle with the Haskell Indians, for a price, of course. Rothstein had no difficulty guaranteeing each player the same amount he had paid the Chicago White Sox players, five hundred dollars.

So, as Coach Frank McDonald envisioned shaking loose Osage oil money for his stadium and Thompson and Cokes reveled in taking Rothstein to the cleaners, Rothstein was dreaming of turning the tables on the unsuspecting schemers.

Arnold Rothstein

CHAPTER 15 – SNAKES ALIVE!

Thanksgiving had come and gone without the exhibition game being played. McDonald was puzzled by the Pawhuska School Board's brief letter informing him the high school stadium would not be available. No reason was given.

McDonald and Hanley made hurried telephone calls to the other school systems in Osage County but could not secure permission to use any of the public facilities. When McDonald sat down with the volunteer coaches of the makeshift team of White cowboys and oilfield roughnecks they claimed to know of no reason why the game couldn't still be played as agreed if they could find a venue. It seemed to McDonald the opposing coaches were more eager than ever to play the game. Then Raven Who Sings appeared at McDonald's vehicle after Haskell's thrashing of Oklahoma Baptist College in Muskogee, Oklahoma on December 15, 1924.

McDonald had made plans with Raven to see her in Pawhuska after the game so he was surprised to find her waiting at his beat up old car in the Muskogee parking lot. She was bundled up in a full-length white ermine coat with matching hat and white calfskin boots and gloves. She looked to Frank like a beautiful brown-skinned snow angel. Frank was unable to get out any more than, "Raven?"

"Frank, we must talk now. Can you ride with me to Pawhuska and let one of the players drive your car?"

"Uh, sure. What's the problem? Is Titanic okay?"

"He's fine. We need to get going right a way."

Frank gave the key of his shopworn old Model T Ford to John Levi's younger brother George and told him to have the team caravan follow Raven's 1924 Duesenberg Model A the hundred miles to Pawhuska.

As Frank sank into the hand tooled leather seat and looked at the assortment of gauges in the sleek and powerful touring car he said, "Raven, isn't this the same model Tom Mix drove to lead the Dewey, Oklahoma Rodeo Stampede parade? You know, my car's named after the alphabet too, but it's a 1918 Ford Model T!"

"Frank, my father and Hubert Cokes have found out why the schools will not permit the use of the public school stadiums. It turns out Arnold Rothstein has hired members of the Kansas City Cowboys professional team to play with the pickup team against your Haskell Fighting Indians. Rothstein has thousands of dollars bet on the game and someone informed the schools your exhibition was turning into a snake pit of gamblers and grifters. The schools refuse to condone it. In fact, if they did allow their stadiums to be used, the high school athletic association would ban them from all league play next year and maybe for years to come."

"That two-bit four flusher! Somebody's going to put a bullet in him someday. Haskell needs this game. Do you have any idea the schedule we put these kids through traveling for days, no time to practice, sleeping in our cars, wearing sweaty jerseys, eating on the road, missing weeks of classes? My god, are they ever going to be treated like the White kids?"

"Frank, do not give up yet. Ti wants to talk with you and Coach Hanley at the Duncan Hotel as soon as we get to Pawhuska. He and Cokes have a fall back plan they want to run by you. When we get back to Osage County can you and Hanley come to the poker room on the second floor and talk to Father and Hubert?"

"Pull over. I'll have Hanley ride with us and tell the players to check in at the Osage Agency with Assistant Indian Agent Violet Willis who is making arrangements for them to stay with Osage families around town. If there's a way to save the game and maybe skin that snake Rothstein, I want to get right on it!"

CHAPTER 16 – KNIGHTS OF THE POKER TABLE

Coach Dick Hanley turned the brass knob on the door to the poker room on the second floor of the Duncan Hotel in Pawhuska, Oklahoma and stepped into the dim opulence that exuded opportunity. Raven held Frank McDonald back by squeezing his hand. Just as Hanley passed into the dazzling light of the chandelier Raven stretched up and bussed Frank's cheek as she whispered, "It will be okay".

Frank was so surprised and excited by Raven's kiss he didn't notice there were four men sitting at the poker table until Titanic Thompson asked Raven to leave them. As she closed the door McDonald and Hanley were invited to sit.

"Do you want a drink or a cigar?" asked Hubert Cokes whose lean bald head reflected the glow from the ornate overhead light. McDonald politely declined but Hanley accepted a tumbler filled with Prohibition whiskey and ice.

"Are either of you gentlemen baseball fans?" Thompson now led the conversation as he nodded toward the younger of the other two men at the table.

"Sure we both are and I think I know who this young man is. Aren't you Pepper Martin, the professional baseball player?"

Martin gracefully rose from his chair, extended his large right hand to McDonald and laconically said, "Hello. Do not let my new team in the Texas League know, but after my Oklahoma City professional baseball team folded this summer I contacted this fellow – indicating the fourth man at the table – and played with his professional football team, the Ouray Indians, until their season ended in New York last week.

"I am a baseball player but I got my nickname, The Wild Horse of the Osage, not from head first slides, but from running the football. You might ask Mr. Thorpe here if that moniker is justified."

McDonald and Hanley were speechless as the man the King of Sweden had called the greatest athlete in the world slowly unfolded his powerful body and said, "I'm Jim. Mr. Thompson and Mr. Cokes asked me to sit down with you about your football game. Shoeless Joe Jackson stood by me when my Olympic medals were taken away and I do not like Arnold Rothstein. Pepper and I are here to help. You know before moving on to Carlisle Indian Institute in Pennsylvania, I attended Haskell. I am still a Fighting Indian at heart. Pepper and I are Indians born and bred and we want Haskell to get that new stadium."

Titanic Thompson said, "Everybody please sit back and relax. Let me bring you up to date on the situation and tell you a plan Hubert and I have put together to save the game and the stadium. Chief Fred Lookout was approached last week by a member of the Kansas City Cowboys professional football team who told the Chief about Rothstein's plan to run in several ringers on the White man's team Haskell was set to play in the exhibition game. The player's name is Rudy Comstock. He graduated from Pawhuska High School in 1918 and he supports Indian students. He wanted no part of Rothstein's scam, but he kept his thoughts to himself until he could talk with Lookout."

Frank McDonald responded, "Ti, that's all well and good but there's not going to be a game. We can't find a field. The schools don't want to risk losing their accreditation by allowing professionals and amateurs to play together. Plus, there is the gambling problem."

Hubert Cokes smiled and said, "Coach, gambling is not the problem, losing is. Ti and I want to fleece Rothstein and you want your stadium. What we need to do is draw Rothstein into a game where he thinks he has fixed the odds but, in fact, we will have. Your John Levi is the best college football player in America but he has now used up his college eligibility and already signed a professional baseball contract, so he's not supposed to play with college amateurs. Pepper Martin and Jim are, also, play for pay. What we propose is a game where these things don't matter, that is, a secret game at a private location. We have found just the spot only a couple of miles from here in Colored Town. Now what we need to do is let Rothstein think this whole thing is his idea and that we are suckers. Ti, would you tell us what you've done so far?"

The poker room door opened as the Colored porter brought in a platter of barbeque brisket, onions, dill pickles and fresh baked sourdough bread.

"Right on cue, Henry. Gentlemen, please say hello to the Reverend Henry Dangerfield, the minister of the Colored Baptist

Church, the unofficial mayor of Pawhuska's Colored Town and the proprietor of Henry's Bar-B-Q Shack just across Bird Creek. Henry got a call to go to Mr. Rothstein's room last night. I had alerted him to let me know if Rothstein was making a move and I asked Henry to suggest to Rothstein that the game be played in Colored Town. Rothstein inquired about a secluded flat field without sandstones where a football game could be played. As Henry and we had agreed he suggested the open area surrounded by homes of Coloreds where the church has its weekly camp meetings. Henry offered the space for free if the church could sell barbeque to the spectators. Rothstein then had Henry bring Cokes and me an offer. Here it is."

Thompson unfolded a sheet of Duncan Hotel stationary and began to read aloud.

CHAPTER 17 – I'LL SEE YOURS AND …

Arnold Rothstein's note was addressed to "My Esteemed Friends, Titanic Thompson and Hubert 'Daddy Warbucks' Cokes". The note offered "the opportunity" for the Haskell Indian Institute's Fighting Indians to meet a team of "hard-working White cowboys and oilfield workers" from the nearby town of Fairfax. The game would be played close to Christmas Day at a field prepared by Rothstein's agents and located across Bird Creek just south of Pawhuska's city limits. Barbeque would be available for purchase. A friendly wager of ten thousand dollars would be placed on the White team if Thompson and his "entourage" cared to partake.

Upon receiving the bet, Thompson and Cokes set right to work contacting Jim Thorpe, a young bootlegger named Charles Arthur Floyd from Shawnee, Oklahoma, and retired United States Marshall Frank (Pistol Pete) Eaton. They secured Thorpe's participation along with the running back, John "Pepper" Martin (The Wild Horse of the Osage) and piqued Pretty Boy Floyd's interest by mentioning the illegal booze concession could be worth thousands, in which Thompson and Cokes would share.

Of course, Marshall Eaton, who now lived in the hamlet of Gray Horse between Pawhuska and Fairfax, was essential to keeping any purveyors of the Volstead Act at bay and making sure Rothstein didn't welsh on his bets. Thompson knew Eaton had grown up near Haskell Indian Institute in Kansas and that he was an avid football fan. Oklahoma Agricultural and Mechanical College in Stillwater,

Oklahoma had just last year (1923) adopted Pistol Pete to be their sports mascot, a point of pride for Marshall Eaton who was famous for his job with the Hanging Judge, Isaac Parker, in Ft. Smith, Arkansas. Eaton had agreed to officiate and safeguard the gambling stakes for a percentage of the alcohol sales.

It took them several days of frantic telegrams and telephone calls, but once everything was in place Titanic Thompson and Hubert Cokes had Henry Dangerfield carry their response to Rothstein:

"To Arnold Rothstein, well known entrepreneur:

If Haskell's coaches agree, we will field a team against yours at your venue on or near Christmas Day if we can select the officiating crew and have the beverage concession and if all involved are sworn to secrecy. Because we know your sporting nature we offer a bet of $100,000 dollars on Haskell with retired United States Marshall Frank Eaton to hold the cash only stakes. The favor of your response is requested forthwith. We would not insult you with a smaller wager."

Rothstein simply signed his name to this note and had Henry return it immediately to Thompson and Cokes. Rothstein was salivating due to his having already provisionally hired eleven members of the Kansas City Cowboys professional football team willing to play if the game took place. Rothstein was disappointed the Kansas City player he wanted most, Rudy Comstock who was from Pawhuska, had not responded to his $500 offer, but he was confident his team of proven professionals would beat the school boys from Haskell.

CHAPTER 18 – A TROJAN HORSE

Titanic Thompson secreted Jim Thorpe and Pepper Martin at Chief Lookout's ranch until game time. But neither Thompson nor Cokes expected help from inside the Kansas City Cowboys themselves. Haskell's team received an early Christmas gift from two of Osage County's most famous football players who were part of the Kansas City organization but whose loyalties remained with the Indians.

After Rudy Comstock graduated from Pawhuska High School, he had been recruited by the Kansas City Cowboys but ended up signing with the Canton Bulldogs. He had spent a month with the Cowboys learning their players and their offensive and defensive systems.

Another favorite son from the Cherokee Strip of Oklahoma was Kansas City's star defensive tackle, Steve Owen. 1924 was Owen's first year with Kansas City. He saw Rothstein's under-the-table payouts to his teammates as disgraceful. Comstock and Owen had returned to Comstock's home in Pawhuska after Kansas City's season ended in December 1924 to see if Haskell might want their help.

"Are you serious?" asked Frank McDonald when Comstock and Owen knocked on his and Hanley's hotel room door on December 15, introduced themselves and offered their services.

Owen, who later became one of the National Football League's Hall of Fame coaches replied, "Rudy and I know the ringers Rothstein has lined up and we know the plays and defenses they like to run. On top of that, we have kept quiet about our feelings so no one knows we are for Haskell."

Comstock said, "We can't help you with the amateurs they will have to use to fill their roster. They may have some pretty salty players who just didn't catch on with a professional team. But we can fill you in on the guys from the Cowboys. They have some good players who swept up the extra Christmas cash. They will play hard, especially when they see us across the line."

McDonald and Hanley were not sure enough about Comstock and Owen to immediately tell them Jim Thorpe and Pepper Martin were going to play. Perhaps this was a ploy by Rothstein to infiltrate Haskell. McDonald suggested the four of them go to the Duncan Hotel's coffee shop and discuss things. Comstock and Owen agreed.

In the coffee shop McDonald ordered a Coca-Cola in the new contour glass bottle. When it was served he opened the conversation with a casual aside, "Gentlemen, did you know this little bottle has helped make Coca-Cola famous? They get these from the Root Glass Company in Terre Haute, Indiana. Funny the useless information we carry around in our heads. Speaking of which, what's this new A-formation offense and umbrella defense Kansas City used a time or two this season? What are they and where'd they come from?"

Owen laughed and said, "I think I can help you there as both are my ideas. One reason Kansas City drafted me was to help coach. I offered to install them just this year. Of course, because I designed them, I know where the seams are. No offense or defense is full proof, not even mine. I'll work with your quarterback, Egbert Ward, right? And your outstanding defensive lineman, Albert Hawley. They will probably catch on pretty quickly. You see, Rudy and I are Fighting Indian fans. We follow you guys!"

Coaches McDonald and Hanley looked at one another and had the same thought, "There really is a Santa Claus!"

CHAPTER 19 – NOT EVEN THE FIELD WAS LEVEL

The Reverend Henry Dangerfield called an emergency meeting of the Board of the Pawhuska Colored First Baptist Church. They met in the twenty foot by ten foot cement block dining room of Henry's Bar-B-Q Shack located at the south end of Bird Creek Bridge. Henry had Elder Jefferson Gilkey let down the oilcloth that covered the sole window and told Deacon Lincoln Finley to pull in the latchstring on the front door.

Reverend Dangerfield opened with a prayer then called the board meeting to order and said: "Gentlemen, you know I's despise alcohol and gamblin' just as ya'll do. But what we has is an opportunity ta sell enough barbeque on Christmas Day ta finance our church for de whole year. We don't even need ta go ta de camp meetin' area. Mr. Rothstein is paying de young men of de congregation ta prepare our meetin' ground as a field for de football game between de Indians and de White men. Everyone who goes ta de game will have ta pass right beside de Shack and we can sell ta them comin' and goin'."

Deacon Finley sat back in one of the old wooden folding chairs Henry used during the week for customers then loaned to the church on Sundays.

"How we gonna keep our young folk from drinkin' and gamblin' while's we's busy cookin' and servin'? Of course, dee

Indians and White folks won't allow for no Coloreds to be officially involved, but they'll shore enough take our money for alcohol and sucker bets."

Dangerfield responded, "Marshall Pistol Pete will be in charge and we'll ask him ta keep all Coloreds away. A young bootlegger named Charles Floyd from over near Shawnee is runnin' de alcohol. I knowed him from his sales ta the Duncan Hotel. I'll make sure he knows not ta sell ta no Black boys. We can just concentrate on sellin' barbeque, potato salad and baked beans. God helps them what's help themselves and we can help keep all dem riled up spectators from drinkin' on empty stomachs. We better start butcherin' and smokin' meat; Christmas is one week away. We'll leave da gamblin' up ta de Indians and White folks and de alcohol up ta Mr. Floyd."

Twenty-year-old Charles Arthur Floyd was already a savvy booze runner when the famous Titanic Thompson and Hubert Cokes contacted him with the idea of greasing the gambling inhibitions with alcohol. Thompson and Cokes knew Floyd hated the nickname his mother had saddled him with, "My Pretty Boy", so they made sure to call him Charles. The promise of maybe up to five hundred fanatic football fans gambling and shouting in the small area of a Colored camp meeting sounded like low lying fruit just asking to be picked. However, there was the problem of Marshall Frank, Pistol Pete, Eaton. Floyd would just have to take his chances and talk to him directly. At least there were no active warrants for him, yet.

Charles Floyd drove his new 1924 Ford Model T the twenty miles to Gray Horse to see Pistol Pete. Floyd dressed in his Sunday best and carried no firearms. When Floyd walked up to the front porch of the Eaton ranch house, the wiry Eaton was sitting on a porch swing with his hands gently resting on the two Colt six shooters he always carried.

Floyd had heard Eaton's reputation for keeping his guns fully loaded. As Pistol Pete was fond of saying, "I'd rather have a pocketful of rocks than an unloaded gun."

"Marshall Eaton, I'm Charles Floyd. Pleased to meet you."

Floyd stuck out his hand, but Eaton did not move to shake it. Eaton just stared at Floyd with a steady gaze from under his well-worn ten-gallon hat. His handlebar mustache was gray, full and untrimmed.

"Uh, Mr. Eaton, Titanic Thompson told me you were in charge of the big football game in Colored Town down on Bird Creek. I believe it will be next Sunday, the twenty-eighth."

Eaton made no response.

"Well, sir, could I ask your position on the Volstead Act?"

Pistol Pete said, "I don't drink and never did."

"Really, sir, well, I can respect that. But do you have a position on it just in general?"

"Yes, it's a stupid law that's made a lot of honest folks dishonest and a lot of dishonest folks rich. Why do you ask?"

"Well, sir, I have the concession at the game, but I can shore let it go if you think I should."

"Son, I have carried guns since my father was murdered when I was eight years old. Guns and alcohol don't mix. The only guns I will allow at the game are mine. Otherwise I don't give a dried buffalo chip what people do about alcohol. There are too many rustlers to run down for me to waste my time on such foolishness."

"Thanks, Marshall Eaton. I'll see ya at the game!"

CHAPTER 20 – WHAT HAPPENED?

Coach Frank McDonald walked from the ostentatious lobby of the Duncan Hotel in Pawhuska, Oklahoma up Kihekah Avenue past the five story brick Triangle Building that housed over one hundred oil and gas attorneys.

Built in 1915 the "Osage County Skyscraper" stood as evidence of the vast oil and gas reserves owned in common by the Osage tribe.

Immediately north of the Triangle Building was a monument to America's first Boy Scout Den (Troop 33) and the large round bandstand where politicians explained the virtues of White culture as furthered by Indian wealth.

The cold December morning encouraged McDonald to quicken his normally fast pace as he climbed the high hill that formed the north wall of the Bird Creek valley in which various Indian tribes had camped for countless years.

When he reached the top of Kihekah hill McDonald turned to survey Pawhuska below him. The town was awash with White businessmen scurrying between offices, restaurants and the courthouse that was to McDonald's right along the rim of the valley.

Frank sat on the dry brown grass and tried to understand how his modest plan to raise money for a new stadium for his Haskell Indian Institute football team had turned into a snake pit of gamblers and bootleggers. Perhaps he should just leave the game to the grifters and take his players back to Haskell.

"I thought you might come up here. Remember how you dragged me up the hill in front of the courthouse when we first met? I checked with Coach Hanley at the Duncan Hotel and he said you had just walked out looking like you had lost your puppy."

McDonald looked up to see Raven standing over him dressed in traditional Cheyenne garb. He was surprised at how natural she looked without her Bryn Mawr style coiffure and clothes.

"So, what's with the native thing? Are you, also, having second thoughts about the game? Maybe we should just let Titanic, Hubert and Rothstein twist slowly in the wind and head for Haskell."

"If you did that, they'd still have the game and blame the loss on you and your team, or, if they won, they'd cut Haskell out and keep all the money.

"No, I was looking for you to see how you were going to put together a team of school boys and professionals in less than a week. I can help with Pawhuska High School. They won't let you hold the game at the high school stadium, but we can probably use the field for practice if we simply show up after school hours. Forgiveness, not permission, is what is called for. And, if they don't forgive you, so what? Soon we won't need the field anymore anyway."

"But, what about letting my amateurs play with professionals? What about the alcohol and the gambling? Is there an honorable end to this thing?"

"Honor is to be found in Indians standing up for themselves against powerful Whitemen who are, once again, seeking to exploit them. To beat Whites at their own game is the honorable way for your team to 'Make Their Ancestors Proud' as Haskell's motto requires. And, if you pull out, what about the Colored people who can, for once, come out ahead in a Whiteman's world? Would it be honorable to let them down?

"I say, quit vacillating and get as much practice in as you can. The game is about a week away now. I will talk with the new young principal at the high school, Mr. Bean. He is a good man and, what's more, he was once quite a football player. Stop analyzing and get to work!

"And by the way, you still owe me dinner."

CHAPTER 21 – HUMBUG

Arnold Rothstein knew a sucker bet when he saw one and a Christmas Day football game was just not going to happen. With White Presbyterians, Catholic Indians and Colored Baptists concentrating on Christmas, the gate, and more importantly the drinking and gambling, would suffer.

The problem for Rothstein was when he was having trouble finding a venue he had been pressured into accepting a Christmas afternoon game time. Haskell's coaches had maneuvered him into a corner. But Rothstein had since discovered how badly Frank McDonald and Richard Hanley wanted the exhibition game to take place and he knew Cokes and Thompson wanted to maximize their chances to fleece the local suckers.

Rothstein called Henry Dangerfield to his room at the Duncan Hotel. "Henry, I want you to get word to Mr. McDonald that the field cannot be ready by this Thursday. I figure your people could use a few more days to get the food ready to sell. By the way, I will be paying the boys from your church double if they will take the time to make the field completely free of rocks. Anyway, I have inspected the goal posts and the crossbars are only eight feet off the ground plus the uprights do not even extend beyond the crossbars. There's no way you can tell if a field goal is good. They must be replaced."

"Mr. Rothstein, we appreciate de extra money but Mr. Thompson and Mr. Cokes ain't gonna take kindly ta a delay. What about de concession that Mr. Nelson has? Will Marshall Eaton okay a change?"

"Baby Face Nelson has already spoken with Marshall Eaton and told him the game might be Sunday the 28th instead of the 25th. Let me deal with Titanic and Cokes. Besides, this game is supposed to be an exhibition between Haskell and the White players from Fairfax. Surely no one is trying to profit personally."

After Dangerfield left the room Rothstein dressed in a dark three-piece suit, orange silk shirt and blue cravat held in place with a diamond stickpin. He put on the highly glossed shoes Henry had just polished then headed for the poker room on the second floor. He considered taking his derringer concealed in a vest pocket but remembered that Hubert "Daddy Warbucks" Cokes and Titanic Thompson were each known to have killed several men in gambling disputes. Better to leave the meeting having lost an argument than one's life.

"Ti, the field cannot be ready by Christmas Day. I think we could play Sunday afternoon if the Haskell Indians and the White team from Fairfax want. It makes no difference to me if the game goes on or not. I'll just assume our bet is off."

"A.R., Cokes and I went out and looked at the field. Obviously the goal posts need to be changed, but that field is going to be a rock pile no matter how long they work on it. It will be the same for both teams. Let's play as scheduled."

"Ti, Hubert, can I be blunt? You two and I may not give a fig about Christmas, but all these god-fearing Christians do. They are not going to be nearly as generous with their money when sober and most of them will be sober Christmas. I know McDonald and Hanley want the game on the 25th but I plan, and I am confident you plan, to seek numerous side bets. I say to the devil with a warm fuzzy feeling. It's time to let McDonald and Hanley know this game is bigger than they realize. With all due respect, maybe your ward, Raven, could break the news."

Thompson shoved Rothstein up against the wall with his elbow on Rothstein's throat.

"You shyster, leave Raven out of this. Cokes and I will get the game date changed to Sunday. You just make sure to bring $100,000 in cash. And, fix the goal posts. We have a good kicker, someone to kick your team's tails and you back under that rock you crawled out from."

When Rothstein hurriedly backed out of the poker room, Thompson slammed the door behind him. "Hubert, if you'll excuse me I need to talk to Raven right away and have her bring the Haskell coaches up to date."

Raven and Frank sat at the ice cream shop next to the Constantine Theater and sipped a cherry phosphate ice cream soda out of the same tall glass using two straws. Frank wanted to concentrate on his game plan, but found his full attention drawn to admiring the way Raven was able to drink the soda without even a trace trickling down her chin.

"Frank, Father and Hubert have allowed Rothstein to believe he has suckered them into delaying the game so that more of the

Kansas City Cowboy professional players will have time to get here. What Rothstein does not know is that you and Coach Hanley have Jim Thorpe secretly working feverously with John Levi on his kicking game. As you have said, field position will be critical. Also you believe there's a good chance the game will be quite close and that either a turnover or field goal may make the difference. Of course, Rothstein we all believe has no idea that Thorpe and Pepper Martin will be playing. The extra time will be helpful so that Pepper Martin and John Levi can continue working on that special play you have designed that calls for split second timing. The Cowboys will get a little more time to prepare too, but since they have just finished an entire season together, they are already familiar with one another. Our real ace in the hole is the two Cowboy players who, unbeknownst to Rothstein, will be playing for Haskell. Not playing on Christmas will give you and Coach Hanley three extra days to pull it all together."

"Raven, this game is very important to Haskell. I appreciate what your father and Cokes are doing. However, I confess I am concerned their desire to make money on the game might deter contributions to the stadium fund. I guess we'll simply have to rely on Chief Lookout and whatever football gods there be.

"Now on to what's really important. When this game is over are we finally going to be able to concentrate on us?"

CHAPTER 22 – OZYMANDIAS

Frank McDonald sat in the small auditorium as Steve Owen was enshrined in the Pro Football Hall of Fame September 17, 1966. A member of the Hall's fourth class, Owen was almost a charter member along with Jim Thorpe with whom he played in the "secret" game of 1924. Neither man lived to see their induction.

McDonald's thoughts drifted away from the ceremony to the last week in December 1924. Young Steve Owen was five feet eleven inches tall and weighed 260 pounds. "Stout Steve" at twenty-six years of age was a prize defensive tackle for the Kansas City Blues (Cowboys), but his true worth went unrecognized by the Cowboys organization that dismissed his innovative football theories.

Owen's birth in a tiny town in Indian Territory in 1898 and his stint as a professional wrestler under the *nom de guerre* Jack O'Brien, did not lend credence to Owen's ideas.

It was not until he was sold for $500.00 to the New York Giants in 1927 that Owen's A Formation on offense and his Umbrella Defensive Formation were fully implemented. But in 1924 Coaches Frank McDonald and Richard Hanley needed all the help they could get for the Haskell Indian Institute's exhibition game to be held December 28.

With Owen's natural affinity for his Indian friends on Haskell's team coupled with the Kansas City Cowboys refusal to adopt his ideas, Owen couldn't wait to go up against the Cowboys in an off-the-books contest. McDonald and Hanley gave Owen *carte blanche* to teach his game plan to Haskell's young players and to Owen's fellow professional players, Rudy Comstock, John "Pepper" Martin, Jim Thorpe and the newest professional recruit, just graduated Haskell senior, John Levi.

To open up the traditional single wing offense played by the Cowboys, Owen put four offensive linemen on one side of the center and only two on the other. The quarterback, fullback, halfback and tailback were aligned so that the center could snap the ball to any of them which allowed for any of the four to run or pass. This "A" formation was named such because it was Owen's favorite of several offensive formations, none of which the Cowboys would give serious consideration.

On defense, instead of lining up nine men on the line with two defensive backs, Owen had the defensive ends and the center drop back for pass plays and stay on the line for runs. This approach presaged modern defenses and resembled an upside down umbrella. The Cowboys' traditional passing offense would find no open receivers against Owen's "umbrella" defense.

Owen planned to have John Levi, Pepper Martin and Jim Thorpe play in the offensive backfield with George Levi who was a sophomore at Haskell. All four could run the ball and catch a pass. In addition, Thorpe and Levi could pass the ball fifty yards on a line. Owen at offensive and defensive tackle and Comstock at guard on both sides of the ball would anchor the blocking and tackling.

Owen's trick play of having the ball centered to any of the four backs who would initially charge toward the line then lateral the ball back to one of the other three for an outside run or a pass was the origin of the modern "flea flicker" and a total surprise to the 1924 Cowboys.

McDonald smiled as he remembered his team along with Thorpe, Martin and Comstock secretly practicing for several hours each day at Chief Lookout's ranch.

Others may have forgotten Steve Owen, but McDonald never would. The final play of the December 28, 1924 game was as fresh in his mind in Canton, Ohio as it was in Osage County, Oklahoma that yesterday forty-two years before.

CHAPTER 23 – BATTLE OF THE WASHITA

Tomorrow's game was closing in on Frank McDonald. It was one thing to have his Indian schoolboys play an exhibition football game against local ranch hands and oil field workers. How could they withstand a no-holds-barred assault by professional players? Losing might be the least of their casualties.

McDonald called for the Duncan Hotel porter, Henry Dangerfield, and gave him a note for Raven:

"I know it's late, but can you meet me in the lobby?"

Dangerfield returned with a response:

"Fifteen minutes."

Raven exited the elevator wearing a full-length powder blue robe over a white silk nightgown that covered her graceful brown neck up to her smooth, angular face. Her long black hair was tied back with a blue satin ribbon interlaced with white. As she stepped out into the lobby her white, beaded moccasins made no sound.

"Hello, Frank. Your message sounded urgent."

"I just needed to talk things through. Hanley was already asleep and my team had better be. Do you have some time for me?"

"If you want privacy, why don't we repair to my room? Henry just brought me a carafe of a rather pedestrian merlot along with a tray of brie and toast. Do you mind coming to my place? I feel somewhat awkward out in public in my nightgown, but I thought time might be of the essence."

Frank did not trust himself to reply so he just nodded toward the elevator.

"Henry, please take us to the third floor. If my father or Mr. Cokes ask you to have me go to the poker room, please tell them I am indisposed."

Raven's suite had a drawing room with a Victorian horsehair chaise lounge next to a small round mahogany table upon which was a carafe of wine, two crystal goblets and a tray of dainty cheese bites on dry toast. Her bedroom could be seen off to one's left from the front door. A large four-poster bed with a lacy canopy was covered with a white silk bedspread and sheets. The covers were turned back and a small chocolate truffle was on each fluffy pillow.

Frank blurted out, "It's no wonder you are so trim. There's not enough food there to keep a bird alive."

"Well, Coach McDonald, there's enough here to keep this Raven alive. What's more there's enough to share. I know you don't normally imbibe, but since the big game is tomorrow, would you care for a glass of wine? Please sit beside me on the chaise. What is so troubling you are unable to sleep?"

"Raven, when I started this fundraising scheme I saw it as a chance for my boys to celebrate after a hard season of endless travel. The kids don't get much support and they have all been removed from their families and homes. We have Indians from numerous tribes spread out over several states. I was just hoping to showcase

80

their talents and get them the stadium they deserve. Instead, I have let this thing grow like a Hydra-headed monster. What if some of them get hurt? You know we don't have a Chinaman's, excuse me, an Indian's chance, against a White professional team. They are going to be embarrassed and it will be my fault."

"Frank, I told you my parents were killed by a tornado. I did not tell you my mother was a Cheyenne named Measure Woman and my father a Cheyenne named Standing Bird. In the Whiteman's world my family went by the last name Bird. My father's older brother was Red Bird who at age eighteen held off Custer's soldiers at the Battle of the Washita in western Oklahoma on November 27, 1868. He was killed but his bravery allowed my five-year-old mother and father to escape. My parents later married and when I was born I was named Raven Who Sings in Red Bird's honor.

"We Indians are used to heavy odds against us when we deal with Whitemen. Your players like football but they love the opportunity to compete against Whites. Tomorrow there will be no bullets, no massacre, no Custer. If we lose the game, we will still win because Indians will be treated as equals on the battlefield and there will be no treaties to worry about.

"You have done a good thing for your players. Their glory will come not from winning, although who says they can't, but from knowing their worth as men who are once again warriors.

"My advice is to quit wringing your hands in self-doubt and get to work on your pre-game pep talk. I suggest you start by reminding your Fighting Indians of Haskell's motto:

'MAKE YOUR ANCESTORS PROUD TODAY'

"Now, thanks to you, they will have the opportunity to do so."

CHAPTER 24 – MAKE YOUR ANCESTORS PROUD TODAY

Frank McDonald had his Haskell Fighting Indians dress in their worn game day uniforms and walk with him from the parking lot of the Duncan Hotel one mile east along Main Street to its intersection with Lynn Avenue then south across the Bird Creek Bridge to the dirt road leading into Colored Town. It happened as McDonald thought it might. All along Pawhuska's broad Main Street Osages cheered the young team and many followed behind as the crowd worked its way to Colored Town.

They arrived at the makeshift field at ten a.m., Sunday morning, December 28, 1924. The late December day had broken with a rare Osage County, Oklahoma drizzling rain that froze on the lank black hair of any Haskell player who chose to occasionally remove his leather helmet.

Coach Hanley and Frank had war-gamed every aspect of the contest. In games against college powerhouses they would be searching for a winning edge. A trick play. A disconcerting Indian war whoop. How to capitalize on the unique characteristics and talents of young Indian men dragged from their Neolithic culture and pitted against young White men who think of all Indians as terrorists?

But in this *ultra vires* struggle against mature professionals playing for money instead of school pride, McDonald and Hanley were concerned with possible serious injuries, probable psychic trauma and almost certain embarrassment. This game called not for an edge, but help from Wah'Kon-Tah.

Game time was two p.m. Four hours to familiarize everyone with the pathetic field, ground rules as agreed between Rothstein and McDonald and Pistol Pete's inscrutable hand signals indicating penalties and time periods. At least Pete planned to signal the beginnings and endings of each period with a shot fired into the ground, not the air. Maybe there would be no ricochet off one of the ubiquitous sand rocks. Of course, if the Marshall got excited his determination to stay in firm control might result in both of his six guns being deployed enfilade.

McDonald told his team to relax until he and Hanley returned from the pre-game meeting with Pretty Boy Floyd, Titanic Thompson, Cokes, Rothstein, the captain and player coach of the Cowboys, the great LeRoy Andrews, and Marshall Frank (Pistol Pete) Eaton at the center of the vacant lot that was to serve as a field.

Rothstein and Thompson exchanged valises with $100,000 in cash that each man counted in front of Marshall Eaton who placed both bags behind him during the meeting.

Floyd's men were already selling illegal booze in prodigious amounts to early arriving spectators.

As Hanley and McDonald slowly walked from the parking lot of Henry's Bar-B-Q up the rutted frozen mud path through Colored Town, Frank saw one-room clapboard and tar paper shacks on each side. Most had no porches and only a sandstone step separated the world from the clamoring children who tried to peer out without being seen. A few of the shacks had front porches made by propping sheets of tin up with saplings resting on stacked stones.

The field was more like a trapezoid than a rectangle because the church members used the south end for a pine wood pulpit for the Reverend Henry Dangerfield. The young men of the church had been hired by Rothstein to lime the field at approximate ten-yard intervals. The goal posts were of different but similar heights. Three rough sawn two-by-fours were nailed together for each goalpost.

If a ball went past the north end zone, it would disappear down a steep bank into Bird Creek. Pistol Pete told each team they would have to provide players to try to catch any errant balls.

When McDonald and Hanley returned to Henry's Bar-B-Q they found the Haskell players huddled under the eves munching on sandwiches.

Henry exited the building and said, "Coach, I hopes ya don mine. We's thought yore players might do better if dey could stay dry and eat sompen."

"Henry, we don't have any cash with us. Maybe after the game we can see you at the Duncan Hotel."

"Ain't no need for dat. We's pulling for dese boys. Coloreds and Indians gots de same treatment from such as des grifters and fancy dans. You jus beat 'em at dere own game. Dat be payment a plenty."

It was now one p.m.

McDonald had Hanley address the team first then said:

"Boys, last night I told Raven I feared some of you might get hurt today and that all of you would be humiliated. I was feeling guilty for getting you into this game, but mainly I was feeling sorry for myself. You know Raven is a Cheyenne, the traditional enemies of the Osages. In fact, our team is made up of several tribes who used to fight one another to the death. But now there is a common enemy. No, not White men like Coach Hanley and me, but lack of belief in your worth as men and citizens of this great land. Many of your people just fought and died for America in the Great World War. You and yours have paid your dues. You don't just belong here because you are the true Native Americans, you belong here because of your character and your courage. Raven made me realize I should not be afraid for you, but that those arrogant White Cowboys should be afraid of you. Now, go out there and, let's say it together: **Make Your Ancestors Proud Today!"**

CHAPTER 25 – GET A GRIP

At 1 p.m. on December 28, 1924 Frank McDonald and Richard Hanley had their Fighting Indians stretching and doing calisthenics. The Cowboys purposefully got as close as they could to the Haskell players. The size and age difference were striking. Except for Steve Owen and Rudy Comstock, the Haskell players were years younger and materially smaller. The only equalizer was the frozen mud upon which all players slipped due to the hard rubber cleats on the soles of the high top football shoes. McDonald had told Jim Thorpe and Pepper Martin to wait in Henry's kitchen until he sent for them. Once the game started he could run them in for a psychological and physical boost for Haskell and a shock to Rothstein and the Cowboys.

The larger and stronger professional players had a definite advantage at the line even without the icy turf. However, it was obvious that most of Haskell's offensive and defensive linemen were going to be easily maneuvered on the frozen field. McDonald and Hanley huddled with Owen and Comstock, but other than an increasing fear of disaster nothing resulted.

Raven and Chief Lookout had observed the dilemma and approached Titanic Thompson and Hubert Cokes with an idea. Ti and Cokes were not ones to panic when the odds shifted. They told Raven and the Chief to "Go for it!"

Raven and Chief Lookout got into Lookout's huge touring car and headed for the Osage Indian Agency high on the hill above

Pawhuska five miles from Colored Town. Their first stop was at the home of Violet Willis, the young Osage girl who worked as an assistant to the Indian Agent. Fortunately, Violet was home from church and just setting down to Sunday dinner with her mother and her sister, Daisy.

Violet, Daisy, Raven and Lookout sped to the sutler's store at the Agency where they grabbed numerous pairs of woolen sox, leather leggings with suede soles and red and black woolen blankets. Hieing back to Colored Town they arrived ten minutes before game time.

Raven said, "Frank, the players will have better traction in these leggings as long as the field remains frozen. The sox and blankets will help keep them dry and warm."

McDonald ordered all the players to put on sox and leggings and cover up with a blanket just as Pistol Pete was removing his six guns to start the game.

The Cowboy lineup included several future members of the college and professional halls of fame as well as current all-pro players. Ironically, the two best Cowboy players were Joe Guyon, a Chippewa Indian from Minnesota, and Emmet McLemore, a Cherokee from Wagoner, Oklahoma. Guyon and McLemore had played with Jim Thorpe and his Ouray Indian professional team in 1923. Then they were both bought by the Kansas City Cowboys. Guyon had, also, played with Thorpe at Carlisle Indian Institute before going pro. Thorpe, Guyon and McLemore remained good friends even though they were no longer playing together.

The Cowboys starting lineup was:

Joe Guyon – quarterback;

Emmet McLemore – all purpose back and place kicker;

Elbert Bloodgood – all purpose back and drop kicker;

Obie Bristow – tail back and wing back;

Johnny Milton – end;

Lyle Munn – end;

Milt Rehnquist – tackle;

Jake Mintun – tackle;

Ivan Quinn – guard;

Dick Stahlman – guard; and

Clyde Smith – center.

Reserves were Chuck Corgan, Charley Hill, Glenn Spear and Coach and all purpose player, LeRoy Andrews. The Cowboys played the same eleven on offense, defense and special teams with an occasional substitution for injuries or a special play.

Steve Owen had convinced McDonald and Hanley to implement the ideas he had not, as yet, convinced the Cowboys to use, i.e., platoon and specialty football.

The Haskell offense was:

Steve Owen – tackle;

Rudy Comstock – guard;

Tom Stidham – tackle;

Vance McGilbra – guard;

Peter Nevada – center;

Dave Bible – end;

Henry Jones – end;

John Levi – running back;

Ted Sallee – half back;

Egbert Ward – quarterback; and

George Kipp – running back.

When McDonald and Hanley called for Thorpe and Martin they would replace Ward and Kipp on offense and play drop back pass defense and double safeties.

Haskell's defense, to start, would be:

Steve Owen – tackle;

Rudy Comstock – guard;

Frank Nix – guard;

Clyde Fairbanks – tackle;

Ansel Carpenter – end;

Albert Hawley – center;

Joe Pappio – defensive back;

George Levi – outside linebacker and safety;

John Levi – outside linebacker and safety;

Otipoby – defensive back; and

Louis Colby – defensive back

Jack Norton, Elijah Smith, Dooley, John Scott and Theodore Roebuck would be a part of all special teams and spell different starters each time with Norton to do most of the kicking.

Haskell's players represented fifteen different tribes and came from eight western states and territories. Several would later turn pro.

As Arnold Rothstein relished the startling differences in the teams, he feverishly made thousands of dollars in side bets with wealthy Indian spectators whose hopes had obviously obscured their powers of observation. He almost laughed out loud when Haskell's players wrapped blankets around themselves and started removing their football shoes. Even the participation of Owen and Comstock did not dampen Rothstein's rush to bet far more than he could cover.

CHAPTER 26 – SKULL SESSIONS

Marshall Frank (Pistol Pete) Eaton took off his ten-gallon hat and waved for the coaches and captains to meet him at the fifty yard line.

"Boys, there ain't a lot of penalties gonna to be called as I am the only official. I'll keep time on my pocket watch and signal the kickoff, first quarter, half-time, third quarter and end of game with one shot into the ground. I have already collected all the firearms and Bowie knives and put them in the Colored church under the guard of four sober Colored boys. Fightin' ain't gonna to be tolerated. If you fight, you're out of the game. Gouging, out. No hidden ball tricks. Any questions?

"This here 1924 double eagle gold piece will say who receives each half. Since no one is the home team, the eagle will be for Haskell and the lady for the Cowboys. 'Ere ya ready? It's the eagle. Which way do you Cowboys want to kick? Toward Bird Creek? Okay, line 'em up!"

Frank McDonald and Richard Hanley sent out their receiving team as the Cowboys nonchalantly pretended to be bored. The Cowboy players sauntered to their kick off positions evincing disdain for the smaller, younger and darker Indians.

BANG!

The inflated pigskin boomed off the toe of Emmet McLemore and tumbled out of the north end zone.

When the teams faced off at the Haskell twenty yard line, Rudy Comstock and Steve Owen could hear one of the Cowboys threatening the young Haskell players: "Careful, Injuns. You ain't gonna make your dead Injuns proud. You're gonna meet 'em real soon!"

Owen recognized the voice of Joe Guyon, the Cowboy quarterback and defensive linebacker.

Haskell tried a running play behind Owen and Comstock, but a Cowboy player ran right over the Haskell players Guyon was talking to and tackled John Levi in the backfield.

When Haskell huddled up for the next play, Owen and Comstock could tell the college boys had been intimidated.

"Guys, listen up. Don't let these professionals rattle you. Beat them by ignoring their jargon. By the way, Joe Guyon, the fella who was doing the talking, is himself a Chippewa Indian from Wisconsin. He's just trying to get you rattled. It worked that time. Don't let it happen again.

"Let's run that same play until we get to mid-field. Whatever you do, don't fumble!"

Haskell tried two more running plays out of Owen's A Formation with the ball being centered to a different back each time. Unfortunately, the same result was achieved. John Levi dropped back and punted the ball almost over the Colored church just beyond the south end zone.

The Cowboys were laughing out loud as they lined up for their first play from scrimmage. Joe Guyon tossed a lazy forward pass over Dave Bible, Haskell's right defensive end, to Johnny Milton, the Cowboys' left offensive end. Haskell's right safety, George Levi, made a touchdown saving tackle at the Cowboy thirty-five yard line.

Owen called for one of Haskell's two first-half time-outs.

"Come over to our sideline boys."

Owen grabbed a slate and a piece of white chalk from the equipment bag. "Dang it! We went over this. Remember the Umbrella Defense? Well, run it! Now listen up. Remember how the two ends drop back along with the middle linebacker? John and George, you must start out here, behind our defensive center, Albert Hawley, in the middle of the defense until you see which way the pass is going. Then rush to the receiver. Got it? Okay, no more slip-ups.

"Speaking of slip-ups, it's obvious the Cowboys can't get any traction on this frozen field. Use your superior footage to your advantage. We got these guys right where we want them."

Otipoby muttered, "Yeah, running right through us like the Battle of the Washita."

Rudy Comstock grabbed Otipoby by the shoulder pads and then slapped his helmet. "You want to quit? Get off this field now!"

"Aw, Rudy, I was just mad. I know we can win. Let me show ya, please."

"All right, but you'd better get your tail out from between your legs and show some Indian spirit. As for the rest of you, quit taking those Cowboys head on. Use some side leverage. Better yet, use some brains!"

CHAPTER 27 – BLOOD IS THICKER

Pistol Pete fired his right hand hog leg into the ground to end the first quarter. The college boys had been able to stalemate the much more powerful professionals using their superior traction on the frozen field. On the sidelines coaches McDonald and Hanley could feel the warming sunshine and the thawing mud. They watched as the Cowboys started the opening drive of the second quarter by running for ten yards directly through the middle of the Indians' defensive line.

When the Cowboys reached the Haskell twenty yard line McDonald called for Raven. "Run down to Henry's Bar-B-Q for Thorpe and Martin. They're beginning to move our boys like cordwood."

Raven tore out from the field in a dead run. About halfway between the football field and Henry's she heard a deafening roar. She rushed on to Henry's where she found Thorpe and Martin anxiously waiting.

"Jim, Pepper, Coach McDonald says to come quick. We are in trouble. I think the Cowboys just scored."

Thorpe and Martin left Raven and raced to the field. When they got to the Haskell sideline McDonald told them John Levi had blocked the Cowboy extra point try. The score was 6 to 0. McDonald told Thorpe and Martin to take their blankets and helmets off and make sure the Cowboy players saw them. Hanley was screaming at McDonald to send them in, but McDonald stuck with his plan of psychological warfare. He knew chance favored the better team and even with Thorpe and Martin the Indians were outgunned.

Once again the Cowboy placekicker lofted the ball through the end zone. This time Emmet McLemore's kick went completely over the Colored Baptist Church.

Rudy Comstock and Steve Owen exhorted the Indians to dig in, not give in. But as the Cowboys gained better footing with each warming moment, the young Indians were losing confidence and yardage. John Levi had to punt again. This time he sent the ball out at the Cowboy two-yard line.

Almost immediately Cowboy starting quarterback Joe Guyon faked a pass and ran away from Haskell left tackle Steve Owen and left guard Rudy Comstock for twenty-five yards. Owen saw Jim Thorpe standing on the Haskell sideline.

"Hey, Joe, look who's with your fellow Indians. Aren't you ashamed to be betraying your people? And, what about you McLemore? Thorpe gave you your first pro job. Ain't you feeling a little strange selling out for a measly $500.00? Or was it thirty pieces of silver?"

Guyon looked at McLemore then both tried to avoid the calm brown eyes of the legendary hero of Carlisle Indian Institute, the 1912 Olympics and professional football. More importantly to Guyon and McLemore, Thorpe was their mentor and friend.

The Cowboy drive stalled at the Haskell ten-yard line as Marshall Eaton signaled the end of the first half.

McDonald called his team together on the sidelines. The rain had stopped and the players eschewed their blankets.

"Boys, put your cleats back on. This field will require a more traditional approach now. You've played well. I'm proud of every one of you. Raven, were you able to get some chow and drinks from Henry's?"

Just then Henry Dangerfield and several women from the Colored church arrived with coffee and slices of pumpkin pie.

"Dat's de best we could come up with dat wouldn't repeat on your players when dey run."

"That's grand, Henry. Thanks to you all. When we win we'll see that the offering plate gets remembered.

"All right. This half we'll put Jim and Pepper in the backfield on both offense and defense along with the Levi brothers…"

"Now see here, you crooks. You can't play those two!" Arnold Rothstein was standing beside Titanic Thompson and Hubert Cokes and had been listening to McDonald's half-time talk.

Thompson said, "Rothstein, you just got out-foxed. You're the one who turned an exhibition game between amateurs into a mismatch between professionals and college boys. Now you are crying because we are playing by the rules you came up with. If you want to call off your pros, we will be glad to play it straight. Is that what you want?"

"What I want is a ruling from Marshall Eaton. Pistol Pete, come over here. We have a problem."

Pistol Pete slowly rolled a cigarette with his right hand as he rested his left on his left side pistol. Then he laconically drawled, "Fellows, it looks to me as if y'all are big boys here. I figure fair's fair and foul's foul and it's all the same to me. Now, let's play ball. The second half starts now!"

CHAPTER 28 – REAL LINEMEN

Marshall Eaton looked at the disappearing lime markings on the field and figured trouble would be brewing in the second half. It would take too long to re-lime everything if the game was going to be completed before dark. Eaton called for Rothstein and McDonald.

"How about each of you getting me twenty-one men with bets on the game? We can alternate a Cowboys supporter with a Haskell supporter every five yards and tell them to stay in their tracks till the final gun. That way they can keep each other honest and I can tell where the ball is on the field. I'll just do my best on stepping off the yardage and calling whether the ball crosses a goal line. Get with it! I'm ready to sound the gun for the second half!"

It was no trouble to find volunteers for each side. Eaton lined them up by resting the barrel of one of his six guns on the right shoulder of each of the "linemen" on one side of the field and using the gun sight to point directly at the man on the other side of the field. Once he got them all lined up, he ordered:

"Men, you can watch the game and yell as much as you care to. Do not move from your position until I fire to end the game. Also, not that any of you would mean to cheat, but keep an eye on the people next to you and keep lined up with the fellow directly across the field. And no more drinking until the game is over!"

Joe Guyon and Emmet McLemore approached Arnold Rothstein before the start of the second half and told him they would not play against their old friend, Jim Thorpe. Rothstein was already feeling the pressure from the numerous bets he had made that he could not cover. Now added to the surprise appearance of Thorpe and Pepper Martin was the defection of his two best players. Rothstein was not yet panicky, but he was no longer dreaming about how he would spend his winnings.

"You better give me my five hundred dollars back."

Joe Guyon spoke for himself and McLemore, "When the game is over we'll meet you at the Duncan Hotel and each of us will give you two-hundred and fifty. We already earned the other half. Besides, if you ain't careful, this crowd will tar and feather you if you lose and don't pay up. We all know your reputation. Maybe you'll just run off when the game ends and we'll just keep the whole five hundred."

The second half was more of a hog-wrestling contest than a football game. Deep mud and a slippery football were bigger factors than size and speed. As the game slogged into the fourth quarter the Cowboys' frustration was taken out with illegal elbows thrown into the faces of the Haskell players. Indian blood and an occasional tooth were mixed with the slimy field.

Cowboys player-coach LeRoy Andrews, who took over at quarterback when Joe Guyon left, managed to repeatedly march his professionals into Haskell territory before having the drives stall due to two fumbles and three interceptions. Jim Thorpe, who seemed to always know where the ball would be coming, guided Pepper Martin and the Levi brothers in the defensive backfield and managed to stymie each Cowboys offensive.

However, the smaller, younger, less experienced Haskell offensive line could not move the Cowboys defense. Haskell rarely made more than ten yards before John Levi would have to punt. Fortunately, his punts regularly pinned the professionals a long way from the Indian goal line.

Coaches McDonald and Hanley were beginning to fear the best their team could do was not lose by more than six points. When Pistol Pete called an official's time out and told the teams there were only two minutes to play, McDonald called the Haskell team over and told them they had to hold the Cowboys on the next drive then use the trick play they had practiced.

With the Cowboys moving the ball relentlessly down the field with running plays, Steve Owen and Rudy Comstock hit Cowboys running back Elbert Bloodgood high and low as George Levi stripped the ball from him. It was Haskell ball at mid-field with less than half a minute to play.

Coach McDonald called a running play and had Jim Thorpe carry the ball behind Owen and Comstock for about five yards. Then John Levi's pass was knocked down by the Cowboys' gigantic defensive tackle Jake Mintun. On third down Pepper Martin was stopped after a two-yard gain. It was now fourth down, about three to go and time rapidly running out on Haskell's dreams of a new stadium and Titanic Thompson and Hubert Cokes's one hundred thousand dollars. McDonald hand signaled to John Levi to run "the play".

With all Cowboys expectations on the great Jim Thorpe getting the ball, Haskell did not disappoint. Haskell center Peter Nevada centered the ball to Thorpe as John Levi unobtrusively moved toward the right sideline and George Levi and Pepper Martin hung back behind Thorpe.

Just before the young Haskell line collapsed under the Cowboys charge, Thorpe stopped, turned around and flipped the ball to the future St. Louis Cardinals Hall of Fame third baseman, John Pepper "The Wild Horse of the Osage" Martin, who passed it to the all alone John Levi who caught it and streaked toward the Cowboys goal line.

The Cowboys players quickly recovered and began to chase John Levi. However, Levi was already on the Cowboys twenty-yard line by the time the Cowboys safety, Obie Bristow, was closing the gap by running at a forty-five degree angle directly at Levi.

Just as Levi raced past the Haskell supporter marking the twenty-yard line, the Cowboys supporter at the five-yard line stepped out onto the field to stop Levi. Levi turned slightly to his left and ran right into Bristow at the five-yard line, Bristow's charge drove Levi against the Cowboys supporter/line marker.

John Levi struggled on with Bristow holding Levi's left leg and the Cowboys line marker standing between Levi and the goal line. A pistol shot rang out just as John Levi dragged himself, Bristow, the Cowboys line marker and the ball across the goal line.

Pistol Pete called the teams together and announced Haskell would get an extra point try, but if it failed, the game would end in a tie.

McDonald and Hanley conferred with their team and decided the muddy field and slick ball made a kick too risky. McDonald used a stick to diagram the play he wanted for the extra point try.

When the teams lined up about halfway between the five-yard line and the goal line, George Levi got down on one knee as if he were going to receive the ball from the Haskell center, Peter Nevada. John Levi lined up in the kicking position. Pepper Martin stood to John's left and Jim Thorpe to his right as if to block.

Nevada centered the ball directly to John Levi who put it behind him with his right hand. Thorpe grabbed the ball from Levi and raced across the right front corner of the end zone.

In the melee that followed, Rothstein slithered away toward his inevitable gambling fate as Haskell Indian Institute envisioned the fulfillment of its stadium destiny. Wealthy Osages opened their hearts and wallets in celebration of a long awaited victory over the Whiteman and Raven and McDonald pondered their future.

CHAPTER 29 – WHAT'S NEXT?

Chief Lookout commandeered several vehicles to transport the muddied, bloodied jubilant Haskell players back to the Duncan Hotel before complete darkness set in.

Lookout ordered steaks and clean busboy uniforms for each player and had Raven arrange for the team to stay and shower in several of the hotel suites. The dirty football uniforms, cleats and helmets were bundled up in sheets and stored in the basement for cleaning then to await transportation back to Haskell the next day. Raven, Frank McDonald and Richard Hanley collected the players' belongings from the various Osage homes while the team was getting cleaned up for a supper to be held in the ornate ballroom with its huge crystal chandelier.

Titanic Thompson and Hubert "Daddy Warbucks" Cokes collected the two hundred thousand dollars from the four young Colored men who had stood guard over the money inside the Colored Baptist Church. They gave the Reverend Mister Henry Dangerfield five hundred dollars for the church and one hundred dollars for the barbeque. They paid Marshal Frank "Pistol Pete" Eaton an additional hundred dollars for officiating. They also suggested that Charles "Pretty Boy" Floyd might want to make comparable contributions. Of course, Floyd did not fail to give Pistol Pete his share of the "concessions".

Numerous Osages collected from Cowboys fans on their bets placed on Haskell, but Arnold Rothstein had managed to escape without being confronted by the Indians whose bets he could not cover. He was never seen again in Osage County. However, he would welsh on his gambling debts one too many times a few years later in New York City.

The proud and happy Indians pledged many thousands of dollars to the Haskell Football Stadium Fund. Only two years after this clandestine contest, one of America's premier college programs would finally have a real stadium in which to play their football games.

Late in the evening of December 28, 1924 Raven Who Sings and Coach Frank McDonald eased away from the revelry at the ballroom.

"I suppose I could've allowed the boys to have a drink or two, but I have always vowed to myself to take care of these kids as if they were my own. I wouldn't want a son of mine to break the law even if it is a stupid law."

"Frank, there is plenty of boozing taking place among the adults, Indian and White. There's no need to subject the Haskell players to criticism and maybe discipline for the sake of well intentioned but overzealous fans who do not have your responsibility. It was a great game. The boys are already sky high. They don't need chemically induced intoxication. What's next for them?"

"Actually, Raven, I was just having similar thoughts. What's next for us?"

CHAPTER 30 – EPILOGUE

Ceremonial entryways have raised human spirits as long as we Homo sapiens have existed. It is likely that one hundred thousand years ago our ancestors erected archways of willows or saplings to mark their cave openings after a successful hunt. Conquerors have a penchant to use arches to proclaim their victories.

Haskell Indian Institute used the 1924 football victory over White professionals to raise many thousands of dollars of contributions from proud Indians to build a new stadium with its impressive archway that commemorates Haskell's football prowess and service by Native Americans in World War I.

As stated by author Myriam Vuckovic in *Voices from Haskell* at page 157:

> **"[H]askell's successful football team and star athletes such as John Levi had sparked great ethnic pride among Haskell's students and across Indian communities. To Haskell's athletes, the football field was a place where they felt they could fight their white opponents on equal terms .... To them, Indian-white football was not just a game. It was about crossing and defending boundaries, history and myth ...."**

Gentle Reader, if you have followed this tale from the beginning, you may have surmised that much of the facts have been shrouded in the mist of hyperbole and faulty memories. There is no doubt this great game took place. But I have related it as I would like to believe it unfolded based in large part on the available research such as sparse news accounts.

The game was played in 1924 at a now forgotten secret location on the tallgrass prairie in Osage County, Oklahoma. There was a great deal of money wagered. Indian pride among wealthy Osages and numerous other Native Americans resulted in generous contributions to the stadium fund.

And, not coincidentally, the Indians did win with two-time All American, John Levi, and future Baseball Hall of Famer John "Pepper" (The Wild Horse of the Osage) Martin playing heroic roles, albeit in violation of the collegiate and professional rules. In fact, it was the restrictions of these rules that required a secret game.

Now, what about this story is myth? Well, frankly, I am not sure even though I wrote it. Did Jim Thorpe play? Some say yes, but anonymously. Did Titanic Thompson, Hubert (Daddy Warbucks) Cokes, Arnold Rothstein, Charles (Pretty Boy) Floyd and Deputy Marshall Frank (Pistol Pete) Eaton get involved? I do not know for sure, but I do know Titanic Thompson and Hubert Cokes spent a great deal of time in Osage County during the 1920's trying to separate folks from their money.

Chief Fred Lookout was actively involved as were numerous other Osages. However, that pretty Cheyenne girl from Bryn Mawr, Raven Who Sings, reminded me of some of the girls I grew up with on the Osage Nation.

I hope you enjoyed the game.

Victory Arch at Haskell Stadium

Photo by Peg Redwine

"The Haskell Stadium was made possible by the gifts of over one thousand Indians representing more than fifty tribes. Every cent contributed in the erection of this structure has come from Indians. It is the largest and most unique Indian project ever attempted, and will stand as a monument built by the older Indians for the younger Indians yet to be educated at Haskell Institute."

Photo by Peg Redwine

Other JPeg Ranch Publications

By James M. (Jim) Redwine:

JUDGE LYNCH!

GAVEL GAMUT GREETINGS FROM JPEG RANCH

JUSTICES OF THE INDIANA SUPREME COURT
    (Published by the Indiana Historical Society Press in cooperation with the Indiana Supreme Court: Contributing Author)

Watch for the sequel to JUDGE LYNCH!
Coming soon: UNANIMOUS FOR MURDER

By Margaret A. (Peg) Redwine:

JPEG RANCH STARZ - Original Felted Creations